TRUE CRIME USA

REAL CRIME CASES FROM THE
UNITED STATES

Adrian Langenscheid

CONTENT

TRUE CRIME USA
REAL CRIME CASES FROM THE UNITED STATES

About this book:
Cold-blooded murders, a tragic kidnapping, ruthless economic crimes, devastating family tragedies, and a spectacular robbery - fourteen true crime short stories about real-life American crime. Neither the judges, the prosecutors nor the defense attorneys are immune to the fact that the suspects are on trial for extremely cruel crimes while the shattering fates of the victims and their families gradually play out. In an ideal world, the final sentence ensures a just punishment for the perpetrators...in an ideal world.

About the author:
Adrian Langenscheid is an author, composer and educational film producer. His work crosses several disciplines and is largely devoted to the narrative of the human experience and the meaning of life. Adrian's passionate True Crime debuted in June 2019. That same month, the book "True Crime

Deutschland", by the as-yet-unknown writer, became a number one bestseller on the Amazon charts
under the category of murder. Adrian lives with his
wife and children in Stuttgart, Germany.

Imprint (German)

Authors: Adrian Langenscheid & Alexander Apeitos
ISBN: 9781676572503

Edited by Jenny Sholer

1st edition Dezember 2019
2019 Stefan Waidelich Dachenhäuserweg 44.71101 Schönaich
Printing house: Amazon Media EU S.á r.l., 5 Rue Plaetis, L-2338,
Luxembourg
Cover Picture: © Canva
Cover design: Pixa Heros Stuttgart

FOREWORD

If you had told me before the publication of my first book that it would become a bestseller within just 3 weeks, I wouldn't have believed you. Months later, thanks to numerous readers, my debut is still on the True Crime Bestseller List. As a writer, the unexpected success has made me humble. It certainly wouldn't have been possible without all the readers who shared my passion for True Crime leaving reviews on Amazon. Only through these reviews is it possible for us lesser-known authors, who have no big marketing budgets or publishers behind them, to be found on Amazon. With "True Crime USA", you now have the follow-up to the bestseller. I dedicate it with gratitude to everyone who contributed to the success of the first book with their purchase, feedback and reviews.

Yours, Adrian Langenscheid

INTRODUCTORY REMARKS

I am a passionate True Crime reader and I love listening to podcasts about true crimes. What I like most is the retelling of real crime stories. I am often deeply-affected with what people are capable of. What is it about True Crime that fascinates us so much? Is it voyeurism or a primordial human need for security? Is it to be able to assess and prevent dangerous situations to avoid becoming a victim of a horrible incident? I am moved by the questions about how things could get this far at all. Would it have been possible to prevent these deeds and if so, who had the power at what time to turn the terrible fate over? Many of these questions often remain unanswered.

Life sometimes writes stories that leave protagonists and viewers stunned and shocked. This is not a story, however. It is cruel reality that will strike you in the next 14 chapters. A reality that is more shattering than any fiction. What happens in front of our own doorsteps can be absolutely incomprehensible and horrifying. It´s about friends and loved ones, the nice family from next door, self-sacrificing mothers or the neighbour who always greeted us in such a friendly and courteous way or people we think we know. But behind their bourgeois appearance are unspeakably deep abysses which nobody, even in their immediate surroundings, would have thought to be possible.

Terrible crimes cause the world to collapse for victims and all those close to them.

Is it really true that the vast majority of all crimes are committed out of passion? Is it true that, under certain circumstances, each of us is capable of killing another human being? By reading the following stories, you can form your own opinion.

In this book, I once again introduce you to 14 famous, real-life, criminal cases, this time from the United States, that happened not so long ago. Let yourself be carried away, touched and moved to tears by eleven cruel, but completely different, murders, a dramatic kidnapping and a spectacular robbery! Feel the almost-unimaginable pain of the victims and their relatives! Experience the screaming injustice of when the perpetrator cannot be identified, and an innocent person takes his place in the electric chair. Amuse yourself with a robbery that remains unforgotten still today and led to the most-expensive gay porn in history! Put yourself in the position of those involved and be amazed at how reality can surpass even the most pronounced imagination!

Ruthlessly, I present to you the true facts in short story form. A few of the participants' names have been changed to protect their personal rights.

While it's possible to write whole books about each case, that is not my intention. Short stories are like an unexpected and tragic storm. Before you know it, it has left nothing but destruction, strong emotions and many questions. Here, you will find crimes in short form that make you want to think further.

As you read these stories, you will laugh and cry, be amazed, horrified and speechless.

CHAPTER 1:

Because he is black...

The scene is tantalizing: The door opens and the three of them come in. One of them is a little boy. He literally has to hold the thick Bible in front of his chest. Without the firm grip of the two guards pushing him forward, the child would probably break down. His whole-body trembles, tears run down his cheeks, his lips shake - for this is supposed to be his last walk. The electric chair awaits George Stinney Junior. Soon 5,380 volts will chase through his little body!

Following a frighteningly cold routine, the 14-year-old boy is placed on the execution machine. He whines, cries, and begs the men around him to let him go; but they don't react. Instead, the straps are tied, and the damp sponges placed. How can it be that the staff remain so unconcerned while the child almost faints with fear? When everything is in order, they cover his face with a cloth and tie it up because the execution witnesses are supposed to be prevented from seeing excessively-gruesome scenes.

It is often said that in one's last moments he sees his whole life flash before him. Was it the same for George Stinney, Jr.? Did the child even understand why something so terrible was being done to him?

George Junius Stinney, Junior was born on 21 October 1929. In Sumter, South Carolina, an old, southern state racial segregation still exists, and people have faith in the healing effect of the death penalty because only draconian punishments offer the best deterrence.

The world George grows up in is experiencing a time of radical change: the First World War has been over for only a few years, and the aftermath can still be felt throughout the USA. It is already clear that the economy is about to enter a downswing - one that will not discriminate between the poor and the rich. After George Junius moved, his family finally gained a foothold in Alcolu, South Carolina.

Those days, blacks and whites in South Carolina could still not sit together on a bus. They had to attend separate schools and their perspectives on life were different. Whites saw themselves as the upper class and had difficulty distinguishing between the faces of colored people. Equal rights for all? Such thoughts are so far away; rather, the colored are seen as unsophisticated, drive-controlled and essentially evil. This already seems to apply to small children. "Negros" are second-class people, with no real possibility of happiness in life.

It's 1944 and World War II is entering its final phase, when a homicide frightens Alcolu. The parents of 11-year-old Betty June Binnicker and 8-year-old Mary Emma Thames soon sensed that something must have happened to the two girls because they didn't come home at the arranged time. The more hours pass, the more worried the parents become, searching for the girls. Finally, they decide to call in the local police, who immediately begin a feverish search. It is difficult to speak of success in this context, but the following morning the girls are found – dead in a ditch.

The sight of them brings tears to even the most hardened men in the community. The children's tender bodies lie motionless and rigid in the shallow water of the ditch. The water causes their dresses to stick to them and allows their skin to shine through. Their hair moves back and forth in the flowing current - as do their heads. The most shocking of all? Their skullcaps are a horrifying mixture of blood, bones and brain mass. Betty June and Mary Emma were brutally beaten to death.

For local investigators, it is not easy to tell the parents what happened to their beloved children. After all, they know each other by sight and have been living next door for years. The suffering in the mines is hard to endure when the bitter truth is revealed to them. Betty June's mother needs a moment to comprehend it all. Suddenly, it hits her like a lightning strike, and she faints on the porch while her husband stands trembling next to her with a frozen face. Mary Emma's parents, on the other hand, run up to the gate to meet the men, take each other in their arms and burst into tears. They have been deprived of the sweetest thing in their lives, a stroke of fate they will never get over.

Deeply moved, the investigators turn away and drag themselves back to the city. The inhabitants of Alcolu are waiting in fear behind window curtains. When they see the investigators, they all run out to harass them into telling them what happened to the girls. A feeling of great distress and unrest settles on the small town, for something so terrible has never happened here before. They don't say much, but the news of the deaths of Betty June and Mary Emma is spreading like wildfire. Deeply worried faces and a sense of bewilderment are everywhere. Soon, the first angry cries for revenge and retaliation are heard. How can one live here in peace and tranquility when he has to fear for his children? Who can rest easy when the killer of two little girls is wandering around free? The cops think the same. They too feel the need for revenge once they have overcome their numbness and shock. Feverishly, they start their investigations and interviews, doing everything they can to present a culprit to the public as quickly as possible. They are unleashed and on the hunt!

The 14-year-old George quickly comes into focus for the investigators. He is a cheerful teenager; in the throes of puberty and just beginning to take an interest in girls. Most people in Alcolu know George, but he has two big factors hurting him: his family only recently moved in, and they are colored. George Junius is a black boy, a fact that is already suspicious in this world of segregation. Add to that the fact that the community watched as he and his sister talked to the two girls on the day of their disappearance, and this fact is sufficient to make George the prime suspect in the double homicide. A witness claims that George allegedly approached the two girls because he wanted to have sex with the 11-year-old. The same day the two girls are found, George is arrested. Unfortunately, this also immediately ends all searches for any other potential perpetrators. From now on, it's all about proving the boy's guilt.
The motive for the crime: Allegedly, George wanted to have sex, but because the older girl refused to engage with him, he felt rejected and decided to kill them both.

The police interrogation soon follows but can't be reconstructed because all relevant documents about it have disappeared. What was it like for George to be in a room with three angry policemen convinced of his guilt? Did they threaten or trick him into finally admitting their truth? Did they possibly even become violent? The only thing known is the result - George confesses to committing the murder of the two girls. At least that's what they say. The truth is, neither a written confession nor a record of the interrogation exists; only a few handwritten notes made by one of the interrogating deputies. Neither George's parents nor his lawyer were present for the interrogation.

With feverish haste they proceed and just one month later the trial starts. The composition of the jury already indicates that there is no easy trial waiting for the defendant, as the jurors are all white men. with families at home, and beloved children they want to protect relentlessly and emphatically from such a monster. And Stinney's lawyer? He shines due to his noble restraint. Unfortunately, he does not succeed in building a real defense for his client. Is it because he can't or doesn't want to? Additionally, important evidence is not sufficiently dealt with. In the end, everything seems like a show trial, and in the center stands a completely terrified boy, completely overwhelmed with the entire situation.

George is sitting on the dock, small, anxious and intimidated. He has trouble following the trial and all the arguments. In the end, he is relieved when, after just five hours, all the talk is over. It was thought that the process would take days before a decision was reached, but this afternoon everything happens very quickly.

As the jury leaves the room, everyone is preparing for a long break. Murder case consultations usually take a long time. The audience is all the more surprised when, after only ten minutes, the door opens, and the jurors return. They didn't spend much time on big consultations; everyone is completely convinced that in that little boy, they found the unscrupulous killer of the two girls. And if not – oh, well, that just means there is one less black person in this world. That is how some people think during his time. The verdict is guilty. The sentence? Death by execution using the electric chair.

Does George understand what is waiting for him? Certainly not, but his parents and family, who break into desperate sobs and tears on the benches, do. The unbelievable has happened - a child has just been sentenced to death! George will be the youngest person sentenced to death. Even now, his lawyer remains passive and does not even attempt to appeal the sentence.

The judiciary seems to understand the people of Alcolu's need for revenge and the boy's punishment is pursued without compromise. A mere two months after the conviction, the date for the execution is set for Richland.

On 16 June 1944, the guards fetch the child from death row and bring him to the electric chair without any human emotion, comfort or assistance. He reaffirms his innocence again and again, but the judges and executioners do not seem impressed and act terribly cold. According to procedural instructions, they finally flip the switches ...

Stinney Jr. never had the opportunity to graduate from school, fall in love, start a family or see his own children. He dies an agonizing death at the age of 14.

While many other cases are forgotten, the fate of George Junius has moved people again and again over the decades. His family, convinced of his innocence, has repeatedly made efforts to reopen the case. They were supported by civil rights activists who were also convinced that the trial was unjust and unjustified.

It will be another 70 years before there is any movement in the matter, but all this perseverance will pay off! In 2014, the case of George Junius Stinney Jr. is again examined by a U.S. court - and the death penalty is subsequently lifted! The judge, Carmen Mullen, is convinced that the boy suffered a great injustice from the state. She describes this case as a particularly bad example of how a black person was injured during the time of segregation by the judiciary. In addition to numerous procedural errors, Mullen criticized the shocking speed with which the sentence was handed down and carried out. The boy's fundamental rights were violated. Mullen is also critical of the confession that formed the basis of the verdict. It was likely obtained by blackmail, but in any case, it was untrustworthy.

The rehabilitation of George is a great relief for his family. His 80-year-old sister Kathrine Robinson, a retired teacher from New Jersey, who also spoke to the two girls who were killed, is incredibly grateful. Since 17 December 2014, it is clear that George was innocent!

However, there is still one tormenting question left unanswered. If George is innocent, then on whose hands does the blood of the three victims stick?

CHAPTER 2:

The phone call

T he six-year-old screams out loud in pure horror as the gun suddenly turns on her slightly older sister. Without any understanding of what is happening to her, the gunshot hits her in the back. She collapses like a little rag doll. That's the moment when the six-year-old turns around in terror and runs to the front door. Her little heart beats in her throat and tears drip from her eyes. As soon as she reaches the hallway, the door is within reach!

But then she gets thrown forward. It's as if a huge fist caught the petite girl in her back. She first feels the pain in her back as she is lying on the floor. It burns so much ... As she hears the footsteps, she continues to try to crawl towards the door, but in vain. One hand grabs the child by the shoulder, trembling like aspen leaves, and turns her around. Then the pursuer shoots the girl in the head.

While the gaze of her eyes breaks and her breathing stops, a last, pleading thought flashes through the child's mind: "Papa ...".

On 2 August 1955, John David Battaglia Jr. was born in Alabama. The next few years he moves with his parents all over the United States. He even lives for some time in Germany, because his father was a part of the U.S. Army. After school, John joins the U.S. Marines, a legendary troupe whose members refer to themselves as "leather necks" or "hellhounds". Those who pass here have gone through hell.

John becomes a sergeant and moves closer to his father, who has settled in Dallas. He attends night school twice a week, passes the CPA exam and begins work as an accountant. In addition, the handsome, 1.83-meter tall man with green eyes models.

It's during this time when John enchants single parent lawyer Michelle G., with whom he experiences the birth of their daughter, Kristy, during their marriage. However, in 1987 he divorces Michelle. His excessive temperament has become a problem in their relationship.

In 1991, John finds a new love of his life: Mary Jean Pearle. On April 6th of that year, the couple give each other the yes-word and one year later, rejoice over the birth of their daughter, Mary Faith. Then in 1995, Liberty Mae is born. The happiness of the Battaglia-

Pearle family seems perfect - at least to outsiders.

For behind the beautiful façade, a crisis is arising. Already on their wedding night John showed his true face, verbally abusing and insulting his wife badly. From then on, such scenes were a part of everyday life in the small family, but Mary Jean Pearle endures it for the sake of the children. Only after an especially violent attack, with verbal derailments, does Pearle finally take heart and separate from John. Since he is no longer allowed to live with Pearle, a visitation arrangement for the children is made. Mary Jean doesn't want to take away their father away from their kids. The two girls love him above all else, and John too adores Faith and Liberty.

On Christmas Day of the same year, however, the marital feud reaches the next level when Battaglia comes to see his daughters. He suddenly freaks out and hits Mary Jean in the back of the head. She files a complaint and her abusive ex is finally punished for domestic violence. His probation period is two years. In addition, Battaglia is forbidden to approach his wife or send her messages. Immediately after the pronouncement of the sentence, Pearle files for divorce, which becomes valid in August 2000.

Battaglia, however, has problems accepting the probation conditions. He stalks his ex-wife, terrorizes her with phone calls, leaves hateful messages with nasty insults on her mailbox. He obviously can't put the whole thing on file yet. At the end of April 2001, Mary Jean finally takes heart and informs the authorities about John's behaviour. She points out that he also smokes marijuana - another probation violation.

Mary Jeane Pearle is still firmly convinced that Battaglia's hatred is directed exclusively against her, because even in his worst phases, he only has loving words for his two girls. That's why she allows Faith and Liberty to continue their regular meetings with their father.
But 2 April 2001 is the fateful day on which her conviction will turn out to be false.

As usual, Pearle brings her girls to the agreed meeting point in the shopping mall. The mother prefers to meet Battaglia in a neutral place. But on this day, he seems a bit tense. Shortly before, the ex-marine received a critical phone call which incited his feelings of hatred. The caller informed him that he would go to prison because of Pearl's complaint. However, the policeman assured him that he would not be picked up until after his visitation with his girls so the children would not have to watch it.

Unfortunately, Pearl has no idea. She also doesn't know that he is taking the girls to his flat on the fourth floor in Deep Ellum instead of eating with them in the mall. On the way there, he probably tells the girls that daddy has to go to prison and that it is their mommy's fault. The world collapses for the 6- and 9-year-old girls.

He encourages them to call their mother and convinces them that she is truly responsible for his prison sentence. Two calls and messages from Faith follow, asking her mother to call her back. Pearle is astonished and responds immediately. Maybe she has a vague idea that something is about to go wrong, but Faith's cheerful childlike voice sounds like it always does, until the moment when Battaglia speaks in the background and prompts the little girl to ask. And she does: "Why do you want daddy to go to jail?"

In that moment, Mary Jeane Pearl's blood freezes and her mobile phone almost slips from her trembling fingers. She suddenly realizes that he knows! Then all hell breaks loose!

Pearle hears Faith shouting in horror: "No, daddy, please don't! Please don't do that!" Then several shots are fired … screams … As if stunned, the mother hears everything through the telephone, witnessing how her two girls are shot, executed, by their father. Then, there is a moment of silence.

"Merry fucking Christmas," Battaglia hisses to his ex through the phone. Pearle suddenly realizes that this was revenge for Christmas 1999.
While the mother immediately alerts the police and

races to her ex-husband's apartment by car, perhaps hoping to save the lives of her girls, Battaglia indulges in a relaxed, beautiful evening. It's as if he's untouched by all of this. For him, the murders are "collateral damage". The message he leaves on Pearle's answering machine immediately after the shots are fired confirms this. "Hi, girls. I just want to tell you how very, very, brave you were. I hope you are resting in a better place now and I wish you had nothing to do with your mother. She's evil and vicious and stupid!" As if nothing has happened, Battaglia meets his girlfriend for a drink at a bar. Later, in a tattoo studio, he gets two stabbed roses in his left upper arm in memory of his children, Faith and Liberty. The police then discover him and, after a fight, he is arrested for murder. Numerous firearms are found in his apartment and the two girls are lying in big pools of blood. Faith is in the kitchen. Liberty seems to have run away towards the door, because she is found only a few steps away from the exit. Both were shot in the back to slow them down before their father executed them with deadly shots to their heads. Both girls were used as tools of Battaglia's relentless revenge.

The trial, which begins in Dallas on 2 April 2002, reveals the whole terrible truth. John Battaglia Jr. has a long history of domestic violence. He broke his first wife's nose and dislocated her jaw during one of his violent phases. Furthermore, he had already threatened to do something similar to her seven-year-old son from another relationship. Apparently, the former U.S. Marine had always had a clear propensity for violence towards children.

The verdict is announced after just twenty minutes of consultation and reads: "Execution by lethal injection" This is also confirmed after appeal. Pearle and Battaglia's first wife, Michelle G., as well as Battaglia's first daughter, Kristy, speak out in support of the death of the man who took the lives of two innocent children simply because he wanted to best inflict pain on their mother. For Mary Jeane Pearle, Battaglia Jr. is the worst of all murderers - worse than Hitler or Jeffrey Dahmer. They didn't kill their own children and she stresses that in her testimony in court.

The defense's arguments are based on the fact that Battaglia has been suffering from a particularly severe form of bipolar affective disorder (Form I) for some time now and therefore, cannot be held responsible for his actions. Several experts confirm the untreated mental disorder, presumably combined with a psychotic episode, but everyone is certain that Battaglia was fully in control and knew what he was doing when he murdered his children. This would not be a reason for a milder verdict.

On 1 February 2018, Battaglia dies by lethal injection. Once again, the manic side of his personality gains the upper hand. After the injection, he closes his eyes theatrically only to open them again a moment later and ask in amusement, "Am I still alive?" In the end, he turns to his ex-wife in the observer's cabin and says, "Well, hi, Mary Jean. I'll see y´all later."

CHAPTER 3:

A cruel plan

(by Alexander Apeitos)

A ndreas and Jan A. are brothers from Aalen, Germany. Today, they are both confined to a high-security prison in Arizona, U.S.A.

Andreas was born in 1960 and Jan in 1963. Not much is known about the conditions in which the brothers grew up. What is certain, however, is that both became conspicuous during the course of their adolescence because of a number of criminal offenses.
Professor Frank Schneider, who works at the Psychiatric Clinic of the Heinrich Heine University in Düsseldorf, will later determine that severe brain damage in Jan can be traced back to abuse in his childhood.
While in their late 20s, Andreas and Jan forge a sim-

ple plan to solve their money problems once and for all. The brothers want to go to the United States to find a wife for Andreas. This will be their ticket to financial freedom.

On August 10, 1988, they fly to San Diego, California together with Jan's wife, Susanne, and Andreas' ex-girlfriend, Anke. The quartet stays in a cheap motel and the brothers immediately begin looking for a potential wife for Andreas.

At a nightclub near their motel, they meet Cheryl R. and her friend Trudy W. The two women originate from Phoenix, but are in town to attend Cheryl's brother's birthday party.

Andreas and Jan involve the two women in a long conversation that lasts the entire evening. Using rather bad English, they tell the women that they are in California on a business trip. They claim that professionally, they produce surfboards, as well as import cars for the noble brand, Mercedes. Before the brothers say goodbye, Cheryl and Trudy pass on their telephone numbers and addresses. They invite the brothers to Phoenix and are already looking forward to continuing to get to know them

Two weeks later, Andreas and Jan are headed to Phoenix. Cheryl picks the brothers up from the airport and drives them to their hotel in Mesa.

Shortly after the brothers check in, they leave the hotel to move to Motel 6, a much cheaper hotel. They tell Cheryl they have found accommodations at the Holiday Inn, because it is more-suited to their needs.

Meanwhile, Susanne and Anke remain in San Diego. A few weeks after the departure of Andreas and Jan, Susanne returns to Germany. Andreas and Jan return to San Diego to pick up Anke. Contrary to their initial plan, no affair develops between Andreas and Cheryl, but it does not stop the brothers from getting to know several other women.

On 6 October 1988, the opportunity finally arises for which the brothers had been waiting. They meet Annette C. in a bar. Andreas and Jan pretend to be bank and computer experts, and at the end of the evening, Annette slips her phone number to Jan. Their first date is he following Sunday. This time, Annette brings her friends, Kathy and Cynthia "Cindy" Monkman with her. Bingo.

Andreas immediately focuses on Cindy. He talks to her and dances the whole evening exclusively with her. Finally, he confesses to her that, "You are the woman I want to marry".

After that evening, Andreas and Jan meet regularly with Annette and Cindy. One day, the German brothers visit Cindy's apartment and $100 goes missing. Cindy gets suspicious. She calls the Holiday Inn to ask Andreas if he accidentally took the money; however, she learns from the reception desk that there are no hotel guests with the brothers' names. Finally she finds out that Andreas and Jan are living in the Motel 6. Together with her girlfriend Annette, Cindy goes to the hotel and the two women meet Anke. They are completely surprised and astonished.

Anke pretends to be a good acquaintance of both Andreas and Jan. She tells the two women that the brothers are not there and that she doesn't know when they will be back.

The next day, the brothers again meet up with Annette and Cindy and explain that they have lost their jobs and work visas because of their desire and commitment to spend time with the women.

The girls feel infinitely guilty and offer to help them find a new job, but Andreas blocks any offer. "What should we do then, marry you?" Annette finally asks. "Yes," the brothers reply.

A short time later, Jan moves in with Annette and Andreas with Cindy. Jan and Annette separate after only one week because Annette discovers that Anke is more than just Jan's good acquaintance.

As a result, he moves out and rents a room in a motel together with Anke. Officially, however, they stated that they had flown back to Germany.

Andreas and Cindy stick with their plan to get married. Cindy initially offers Andreas a marriage of convenience to make it easier for him to obtain a work and residence visa, but Andreas swears to her that he wants a real marriage - one that will last forever.

On 28 October 1988, Andreas and Cindy marry in Las Vegas. Neither family nor friends are present at the ceremony, as the two have decided to keep their marriage secret.

Just 10 days after the marriage, on 7 November 1988, Andreas contacts an insurance broker. He is interested in a $1 million life insurance policy for his newlywed wife.

When he tells Cindy about his idea of taking out a life insurance policy, she suspects that this is common among married couples in Germany and agrees. Cindy then takes out a life insurance policy for $400,000 and at the same time, writes a cheque for the first instalment.

The brothers' plan seems to work. Andreas, Jan and Anke immediately start to budget the money. They obtain expensive sales contracts for watches and two Jaguar cars. In each case, they make a down payment and promise to pay the balance when they receive their money from Germany.

On one of these shopping trips, Andreas tells Anke that he would be a rich and made-man, if Cindy were to die an unnatural death.

Meanwhile, Cindy has found a second job to take care of herself and Andreas. He, on the other hand, has no problem spending her money on Jan and Anke's living expenses.

On November 25th, Andreas receives a call from the insurance broker. The insurance company has examined Cindy's application and is only able to cover her for $100,000. However, another insurance company could be used to supplement an additional policy for $300,000 more. Done! The insurance contracts state that the first day on which the life insurance policies can be claimed is December 22, 1988.

On the day after this, i.e. 23 December 1988, Cindy packs her suitcases. The following day, on Christmas Eve, she wants to fly to Illinois, to spend the Christmas holiday with her sister and family. That evening before she plans to fly out, she arranges to meet her friend Annette at 8pm to exchange Christmas presents.

The two brothers are also very busy the day before Christmas, renting an off-road vehicle with a large storage area and meeting Anke at the motel. There, Andreas tells them that they will have a lot of money if he kills Cindy today.

The plan is finalized, and Andreas agrees to pick Cindy up shortly after 7pm. Then Cindy's girlfriend, Maria, wants to pick her up and drive her to the restaurant to meet Annette.

Cindy calls her father around 6:50p.m. and then Maria to include her in the planning. During the phone call with Maria, Andreas comes home, and Cindy ends the conversation.

Meanwhile, Anke and Jan arrive about 7pm at the agreed meeting point with Andreas.

About 20 minutes later, Andreas drives past them. Anke and Jan follow his car towards the desert.

At some point, Jan turns off the road and drives around in the desert for a while. A short time later, Anke and he discover Andreas's car again. Jan stops, orders Anke to stay in the car, and walks up to his brother. Upon his return to the car, Jan arranges to meet Anke back at the bar at 10:30pm with Cindy and Maria.

Andreas and Jan drive to the motel to take a shower and then meet Anke at the bar.

The three officially wait for Andreas' wife for a while, and then order dinner and talk about their alibi. Afterwards, they visit a nightclub until Andreas finally comes home around 2am the next morning.

Cindy's answering machine is full of messages from Annette, Kathy and Maria. They are worried because Cindy didn't show up for their meeting.

On the early morning of December 24, 1988, Annette finally reaches Andreas, who seems just as surprised about Cindy's disappearance as she is. He tells of Cindy leaving the house around 7pm after a heated argument on the phone with a strange man. They were actually supposed to meet at their regular bar at 10 pm, but she didn't show up.

Annette immediately drives to Andreas so they can inform the police together. Arriving at his place, Annette stumbles over Cindy's handbag. The girlfriend is irritated – why is the bag here? Why didn't Cindy take it with her?

On the afternoon of December 24, 1988, Cindy's body is found in the desert of Pinal County, Arizona. She was stabbed once in the chest and four times in the back. Also, her throat was cut so deep that her head was nearly decapitated. Her body and face showed various bruises and the dead woman's forehead contained the imprint of a sports shoe.

A piece of nylon string and a bloodied beach towel are found near the body. Furthermore, clear tire marks and another sneaker print can be detected.

On the late evening of December 25, 1988, Andreas, Jan and Anke drive around the Salt River with the rental car.

Andreas drives fast into the curves and brakes abruptly again and again. By doing so, he wants to damage the tire's tread in such a way that it no longer corresponds to the tracks found at the scene of the crime.

When the car was returned to the car rental company, two tires had been lowered in such a way that they needed to be replaced.

On December 31, Andreas, Jan and Anke fly to Illinois to attend Cindy's funeral. On January 2, 1989, they return to Phoenix, only to fly to Los Angeles the next day, where they pay a homeless person $20 to leave a message on Cindy's answering machine. They provide him with the text of the message, which states, "I slit your wife's throat [...]. If I don't get my things soon, your girlfriend and brother will be next and then it's your turn [...]. My eyes are everywhere."

Back in Phoenix, Andreas brings the tape to a German-speaking investigator who is supposed to translate it. He urgently refers his visitor to the police.

At the same time, the police discover that Cindy took out a life insurance policy shortly after her marriage identifying her husband, Andreas, as the beneficiary in the event of her death. In relation to the presumably false threat on the answering machine, Andreas, Jan and Anke become the main suspects in the murder case.

On January 5th, the investigating police positioned a total of eleven officers around the apartment complex where Andreas now lives with Anke and Jan. Around 8:30pm, an undercover investigator knocks on their apartment door. He wants to make sure that the three are really at home. Andreas opens the door and the officer stammers something along the lines of, "Sorry, wrong door".

Andreas immediately calls the police and reports the strange incident. The next day, he is ordered to the police station to provide a sketch of the man. He doesn't know that it's a trap – which now snaps shut.

Anke and the two brothers arrive at the police station on January 6th. The policemen talk to each of them individually. They let Anke wait alone for several hours in the lobby, until the right moment arrives. Suddenly, the police officers ask Anke in for questioning. They urge the woman to tell the truth about the murder of Cindy Monkman.

If she confesses, they promise her full immunity on all charges. That means absolute impunity. The investigators increase the pressure by repeatedly presenting Anke with photographs of Cindy's brutally-treated body. Anke soon collapses like a house of cards. She confesses to the police that Andreas, Jan and she planned the crime together because of the money from the life insurance policy. The brothers are immediately taken into custody.

On January 9th, the police search Cindy's apartment and confiscate a crossbow, Andreas' tennis shoes and two rolls of photographic film.

A short while later, Anke writes some letters to Jan in prison. These letters further confirm her participation in the murder of Cindy and are confiscated by the police as important evidence. Likewise, a letter from Andreas to Jan, in which he wrote in German, "I met a guy who comes out in 2-4 days and then we'll be free in 1-2 weeks [...]. The police can't do anything [...]."

The brothers are tried separately. In both trials, Anke appears as a crown witness. With her testimony, she heavily implicates Andreas and tries to exonerate Jan by stating she neither saw a knife nor traces of blood.

In the trial against Jan, however, it comes to a decisive turn. An expert, commissioned by Jan's own lawyer, announces in court that the perpetrator must be right-handed.

However, Andreas is left-handed, and Jan is right-handed. The jury is convinced of the expert opinion. After all, he was commissioned by the defense, so why doubt it?

Andreas is sentenced to death by the Superior Court of Arizona on 10 August 1990. His brother Jan received the same sentence on 8 January 1991.

Andreas's first execution date is on June 5, 1989. A

federal appeal procedure, however, results in a post-ponement of the execution. Therefore, Andreas is still on death row at the high security prison in Florence, Arizona.

Jan's death sentence was commuted to life imprisonment by Judge Silvia A. in May 2009 because Jan is proven to be mentally-retarded. The German expert, Frank Schneider, had already classified him as unfit for debt due to brain damage. On the basis of this expert opinion, his lawyer first applies for the abolition of the death penalty and the court granted the application. In his decision, Judge Arellano pointed out that Andreas spoke good enough English at the time of the crime to rent property and take out insurance. His brother, on the other hand, had already attended various special education schools as a child and had been kicked out of the German army. As a result, he became fixated on Andreas.

But how could Cindy fall for Andreas?

Cindy Monkman was born on September 16, 1959. She grew up with her sister, Kathy, and her brother, John, in regular family relationships. When Cindy was 7 years old, her mother died. Because of that, the family grew together even more.

Cindy had just turned 30 when she met Andreas and fell in love with him. She was an open, cheerful and beautiful young woman. Maybe it was the famous rose-colored spectacles that made Cindy overlook the warning signals, or perhaps she just couldn't guess what a perfidious plan she had been drawn into.

Cindy's murder shows how kindness and affection can be ruthlessly exploited. It turned out to be a deadly disaster for Cindy Monkman, a young woman who simply fell in love and felt responsible for unconditionally supporting her beloved partner.

CHAPTER 4:

Lovesickness

I n the '70s, he would have given anything to go to the police. Perhaps this is a reaction to the many upheavals in this particular decade. George Nixon is elected president in the U.S.A. and stumbles upon the Watergate scandal. The Vietnam War claims countless dead and wounded. Hostages are taken at the Olympic Games in Munich and a Polish priest becomes pope. On the other hand, the 70's are also marked by such dazzling things as the hippy movement, flare pants, plateau boots, Bhagwan and the very first video game called Pong. It is also the time of the great movie classics like Apocalypse Now, Clockwork Orange, Star Wars and the highly-unconventional, Rocky Horror Picture Show.

Born in 1955 in Miami, Florida, George Manuel Bosque was fascinated by the idea of joining the police and ensuring law and order. The teenager of Cuban descent is eagerly looking forward to his graduation, after which he can finally apply to become a law enforcement officer. Unusual for a young man in this colourful time are his ultra-conservative views, which is why someone will later even call him a "self-proclaimed Nazi". In fact, George has a big problem with such things as nudity, homosexuality and, as he sees it, the "glorification of narcotics". He literally crusades for his out-of-touch beliefs and writes letters to the editor of the newspaper, strongly condemning these excesses. However, in this era of great, groundbreaking movies, his later fascination for this very medium will play a decisive role in Bosque's life.

After George graduates, he immediately moves forward with his plan to apply to the state law enforcement agencies. When his first application is rejected, Bosque does not give up. There are still so many police stations in the country, as the United States is quite large! He writes and sends, writes and sends... but only gets refusals back. The fact that no one wants to hire him, when he desires so much for the job of the policeman, is a heavy slap in the face for the talented and enthusiastic young man. Eventually, he is forced to admit that no one will give him a chance, no matter how hard he tries. Perhaps this is the moment when George's ultra-conservative beliefs lose their radiance and begin to crumble. For what is he supposed to do if the "normal" people don't support his ambitions? Resigned to his fate, he accepts a job as a security guard at Brink's, a large security service provider in San Francisco, where he mainly transports valuables. This is the closest Bosque can get to his dream job.

Surprisingly during this time, the young man throws some of his strict views overboard. Homosexuality, in particular, suddenly no longer seems to scare him and he falls in love with Carl D., whom he will refer to as the love of his life. George blossoms in this love. It feels like heaven and he enjoys the moment and his life. Toward the end of the 70's in sunny San Francisco with his great love, the young man from Miami enjoys the great freedom that feels like heaven on earth to him. But soon the 80's come, and his happiness ends abruptly.

In 1980, Carl breaks up with him. He probably utilizes the typical phrases like - we just don't fit; it's not working out with us; we're just too different; blah, blah, blah. George is thrown back to earth from his personal little heaven, into the misery from which he came. He is suddenly nothing again, a nobody.

This is the moment when George Bosque freaks out. Something in his mind licks, and he literally goes crazy. Later, he will state that in that moment, many confusing thoughts spun around in his head almost like a wild, crazy kaleidoscope and then suddenly, he just knew what to do. He realized the only solution to all his problems and he immediately went to work. However, Bosque now functions ice-cold and like a machine.

The financial transports of his employer, Brink's, are repeatedly the object of criminal desire, but on August 15, 1980, George succeeds in what many only try to do. He steals his own armored money transport which, at the time of the crime, contained $17 million in funds from Hawaiian banks for the Federal Reserve Bank in San Francisco. That's a lot of money to resolve a lot of personal problems and maybe even win back the heart of his painfully-missing love, Carl?

George is modest. He only takes two bags of $50 bills and two bags of $100 bills. He then settles down with his $1.85 million dollars of "pocket money" and flees to the San Francisco International Airport, where his trail is lost.

What then follows speaks of the lunacy. The people at Brink's are furious about the brazen robbery. They even establish a reward of $150,000 dollars for the capture of their former colleague, George Bosque. Some assume he has left for South America, more precisely Peru. Not only are the cops vigorously searching for the 25-year-old, but the insurance company, Lloyd's of London, which insures the handsome sum, is searching as well. Everybody is on the hunt for George Bosque, but nobody discovers a trace of him. Yet, he is almost right under their noses.

Travelling all over the United States, he is spending the stolen money with reckless abandon.

In his delirium, George lives unleashed and enjoys every single moment. He gives free rein to all the wishes and desires that have ever slumbered within him and which he has laboriously controlled all these years. It's almost as if the million-dollar robbery was the precipitating event to bring the true George Bosque to life. And he really knows how to celebrate!

George appears in Denver, Chicago and Florida, but above all, he appears in New York, where he rises to become an icon of the underground gay scene. And it's no wonder, Bosque is extremely generous and likes to share his new wealth with others. Anyone from friends to charities who asks him for money gets it, with both hands. He will later explain that, "My biggest enjoyment with the money came about when I shared it with other people".

Bosque indulges himself with something good as well. He lives in exclusive penthouse suites and allows himself to be driven around in limousines, helicopters and cabin boats when he needs to travel or simply wants to take a ride. He spends as much as $60,000 to redesign an apartment in Greenwich Village with an opulent art deco style. The apartment rents for $1,160 a month. In addition to modular seating elements covered with elephant skin, he also buys a $10,000 dining table.

George enjoys the beautiful things in life to the fullest. Unfortunately, cocaine is also a part of his new way of living, and not "a line" every now and then, but in substantial quantities. The white powder is actually everywhere when Bosque is around.

At some point, the boredom of the permanent party sets in and he begins to look for a new project where he can do something good for his friends and make him a part of the annals of filmmaking history. Bosque invests a six-figure sum in a porn production - but not just any porn! The gay porn, "Centurions of Rome", is a milestone in almost every way. The raunchy flick for men's fantasies costs the then-exorbitant sum of $200,000 (the equivalent of $600,00 today), of which $160,000 are from George Bosque's personal purse. No wonder, since the cult movie bursts every frame in this genre by numerous superlatives. There are various detailed sets for the scenes in ancient Rome and a total of 32 "actors".

Bosque enjoys his new role as producer quite a lot; but above all, it's important to him that the people on set are also happy. That's why the catering doesn't just include hot and cold drinks and snacks, but also other things to get into the right recording mood - lots of first-class cocaine, free of charge, of course. "Centurions of Rome" will go down in history as the movie in which free cocaine was part of the catering. Daily. Thanks to George, the actors and the crew receive their paychecks on a daily basis, and at the end of each day, a handsome sum of cash awaits them.

Despite these "excellent" conditions, the project turns into a disaster. One reason is the ridiculous dialogues Bosque writes at the last minute before shooting. Moreover, none of the performers have ever sat on a horse before, which is why the numerous riding scenes are absolutely embarrassing to watch. Bosque also insists that scenes be shot in a local fisting club, simply because he is promised a free, life-long membership there.

George Bosque is broke even before post-production starts. Just 15 months after his sensational coup, his new friends are also gone. He finally decides to return to San Francisco to look for his beloved Carl D. What he doesn't know, is that his former lover has moved to Texas. Nevertheless, Bosque's arrival is eagerly-awaited in San Francisco. In November 1981, the police arrest him in the parking lot of a supermarket.

His trial ends in February 1982, when Bosque pleads guilty and is sentenced to 15 years in prison. He was released early in 1986, but only 5 years later, he is back in the headlines when, on 1 July 1991 he is found dead, presumably from an overdose. To that end, the 36-year-old remains faithful to his true love - drugs.

For Brink's, the whole thing has a bitter aftertaste. The FBI was only able to recover $20,000. As a result and in a related court case, an attempt was made to secure the rights for "Centurions of Rome", but when photos of the fisting club were put on the table for evidence, the company thankfully abdicated.

CHAPTER 5:

The tape

W hen, after what felt like an eternity, the very last hissing and crackling of the audio tape finally fades away, the men feel as if they are awakened from an endless nightmare. One of them places his heavily-trembling hands on his thighs to give himself some stability in the face of the horrible recording. Another struggles desperately with the lump in his throat, unable to make a sound. From his throat comes only a weak caw. What he just heard is so infinitely shocking, so cold-blooded, that even the detectives with extreme intensity feel their own weakness and helplessness in this moment.

The cries of the young people, their desperate pleading and crying to let them live, still echo in the heads of the investigators. Then shots and rumbles as they fall to the ground. Shot by a merciless hunter lurking for them in the safety of the darkness. Their deaths have degenerated into a surreal audio drama. A scene in which one can participate live and yet is unable to help. They die because a man commits vigilante justice.

Byron David Smith, a 64-year-old former U.S. State Department security technician, is on the phone. He is extremely polite and humble as he calls the Belle Prairie Community Police Department in Morrison County, Minnesota on November 22, 2012. He wants to report a burglary at his home that happened yesterday. He said he didn't want to bother the police by reporting it on the holiday. Two people were killed in the incident because Smith had to exercise his right to self-defense, he calmly explains.

The cops are irritated. Presumably, it is not so much the fact that the pensioner has made use of his right to protect himself from intruders but rather, the almost cheerful objectivity with which he presents this. It is their duty to go to his home in Little Falls to see for themselves. Smith awaits them at the front door and willingly leads them to the corpses in the cellar that lie next to each other. The pensioner even apologizes for the disorder, as he leads the investigators down the steep stairs and through the gloomy, slightly musty cellar rooms with the worn furniture. After the incident, he had not yet come to clean up, he explains. Then he points to the bodies of the burglars and his voice almost resonates with pride as he tells the policemen about it.

The men step up - and immediately freeze in shock. What they see is hard to believe. In front of them on the floor are the dead bodies of two teenagers, 18-year-old Haile Elaine Kifer and her cousin, 17-year-old Nicholas Brady Schaeffel. Both are familiar faces, but what shocks the usually hardened policemen are their appearances. Both are covered in blood, lying in a dark, thick pool of blood. They are literally sifted with bullets. Was this really self-defense?

Sheriff Michel W. reflects briefly, then goes over to Smith, who is still smiling with a friendly smile and arrests the completely surprised man.

As he leaves the cellar, the sheriff's gaze falls upon an audio recorder near an armchair that cannot be seen from the stairs. It's more of a gut feeling that makes the policeman take that recorder with him. And in fact, it will later turn out to be a significant piece of evidence.

Byron David Smith is well-known in Little Falls. He is a former government security engineer who, during his active time, even travelled to Moscow, Bangkok and Beijing. He lives alone in his home with a large garden, which is far too large for one person, especially when you're not-so-young anymore. That's why in the summer 2011, Smith asks some young people from the neighbourhood if they would like to care for him and earn a few dollars as well. Among them are the unconcerned Haile Elaine Kifer and her cousin Nicholas Brady Schaeffel, who are rumored to have ties to drugs.

Smith is very friendly to the teenagers - he expects them to work hard, but also brings them to his house to eat and drink. Sometimes, he just talks to them. It's probably during these hours together that Haile and Brady get an overview of the interior of the house and Smith's possessions. Perhaps this awakens their desires. Through these visits, Haile and Brady also learn that Smith is a bit odd about his safety. A neighbor will later even call his behavior paranoid. Because the pensioner feels latently-threatened, he has multiple weapons in his home and even installs a security system. Furthermore, he has come up with a kind of "secret code" for the door. Only those who know the special knocking sequence are admitted.

When Smith stops letting Haile and Brady work for him that next year, the burglaries at his house begin. He will later tell the police that he was robbed six times in 2012 before Thanksgiving. In fact, there are indications of two earlier burglaries but, strangely enough, the crimes were never reported to the police. Apparently, the criminals were mainly looking for cash, since a total of $4,000 cash, Smith's father's prisoner-of-war watch, coins from a collection and a chainsaw were stolen.

The pensioner does not report all of it because he does not trust the local police to effectively be able to prevent something like this from happening again. He decides that he needs to take care of it himself. Nobody else but him seems to be able to really take care of the mess. Initially, Smith begins to carry a holster with a loaded weapon around his house. He wants to be prepared when someone appears un-invited in Smith's home. In his basement, he sets up a kind of "headquarters". In this base camp, the security engineer deposits some bottles of water and muesli bars. He wants to be prepared in case he has to spend a long time there, maybe while waiting for something or someone ...

The teenagers are unaware that Smith is setting up a trap. He already suspects them of repeatedly enter-ing his household and instead of demanding justice from the authorities, Smith only wants vengeance. Later, critics even speculate that his plans might have been much more far-reaching and that the job offer itself was already an early part of it.

Haile is a cheerful, unconcerned girl who likes to buy beautiful things. She wants to live and have fun but without money, her possibilities are limited. She spends a lot of time with her younger cousin who likes to occasionally take drugs. Apparently, the small town doesn't offer enough variety for adven-turous teenagers like him. Is it boredom or the desire for thrills that gives them the idea of burglarizing Smith's home? They know him well and they know where to find things that can be turned into money. In fact, they are so confident that the pensioner is slowly becoming a kind of "piggy bank" for them.

On Thanksgiving 2012, the events take place with a consistency that no Hollywood screenwriter could have envisioned more precisely.

Things start when Smith appears to leave his house. In actuality, he sits in his truck and drives off to a neighbour's house. There, he parks his vehicle and makes his way back to his house unnoticed. Smith walks down to his basement, turns out all the light bulbs and takes a seat in the comfortable old armchair in a dark niche that is practically invisible from the stairs. The retired pensioner has a nice book and two rifles close at hand. Sufficient food and drink were deposited there long before. To avoid the waiting time, Smith talks for a test on the digital audio recorder, which from now on, records the events in the basement.

The sentences he speaks to himself while waiting for the burglars will later become an important part of the evidence for Sheriff W., leading him to believe that Smith has been planning his revenge from the very beginning and down to the smallest detail because early on he records his later statement for rehearsal purposes!

In the meantime, Haile and Brady don't know anything about any of this. They don't know that they are being set up for a trap and can only await their terrible consequences. The teenagers only see that Smith drives off and leaves his house. The youngsters consider the whole situation as a perfect opportunity to once again make their own cash register a little fuller.

The 17-year-old Brady smashes a window and first

enters the home. He will also be the first to enter the cellar. The young man feels safe and has the impression that there is enough time to search for something useful. A total of 12 minutes pass before he descends the stairs, where Smith patiently awaits the teenager in the dark with a gun in his hand.

It's almost as if a hunter is waiting for his prey, because when Brady stands on the stairs, the pensioner fires at him twice. He hits Brady both times. Not seeing his attacker, the boy collapses, severely injured and falls down the steep stairs. He lands on his stomach and lies groaning and twitching in front of the old man. But the merciless hunter knows no compassion, Smith shoots him in the head with precision and extreme coldness. Done.

Is it the joy of a successful hunter that makes Smith mock his dead victim? This lasts only a short time, for the man knows that Haile is still somewhere. Therefore, he wraps the boy in a tarpaulin and drags him into an adjoining room. Nothing should reveal to the girl what just happened here.

Smith returns to his chair, reloads and prepares himself for a longer waiting time. The recording device keeps running and stores the thoughts that the pensioner expresses during the whole time. He sees the action as an operation to clear up the chaos. For him, this retaliatory act is his sacred duty as a member of the public, because the criminal prosecution system itself does not seem to be in a position to ensure law and order. "I had to clean it up" seems to be the man's inner conviction as he waits for his next victim - for about 15 minutes.

His body is again filled with icy concentration as he hears Haile calling for her cousin upstairs. A few moments later, the girl is on the staircase. She hesitates briefly because of the darkness , but then begins to descend the stairs to the basement. In this moment, Smith aims at her and shoots. The hit immediately knocks Haile off her feet, and she falls down the stairs in shock. She screams in horror and expresses desperate shouts like, "I'm sorry" and "Oh God!" None of this impresses the self-proclaimed avenger. He fires several more shots into the defenseless girl's upper body as she begs for mercy. One shot grazes her left temple, but she is still alive. Obviously, Smith enjoys mocking her, too, before he throws Haile over his shoulder and deposits her on her cousin's body in the next room. Now he gives his second prey the death shot - directly under the chin.

All this is not only recorded on the audio recorder, but also by the installed security cameras, because Smith believes he is acting completely in accordance with the law. He simply views the whole situation as an emergency response to protect himself from potentially-armed burglars.

However, the jury will see the whole matter very differently. The 2014 trial didn't take long, just 11 days. The jury only needed three hours of counsel to find Byron David Smith guilty. According to several legal reports based on the Minnesota "Castle Doctrine," the first shots taken at the teenagers were legal. However, there is plenty of evidence that speaks equally clearly for intent and excessive use of violence. For example, Smith pretended to drive away and did not inform the police of the burglaries because, in his view, they would not be able to take the appropriate action. Therefore, he exercised vigilante justice. The tape recordings were another important point of reference for the jury, which supported this impression. The verdict finally found Smith guilty on two counts of first-degree murder with premeditation and two counts of second-degree murder without insidiousness.

For Smith, this is a misjudgment of the court, which is why his lawyers appeal to the Minnesota Supreme Court that same year. But the court affirms the verdict two years later. That's no reason for Smith to rethink his view of all the events that Thanksgiving. At the end of 2018, his lawyer appeals to the U.S. Appeals Court in the hope of reexamining his client's case. The verdict is not upheld, but the complaint certificate issued is not a carte blanche endorsing Smith's view. It's overturned because the certificate was issued due to formal errors made in the previous hearing. More precisely, the judge feared that the media would influence the jury in 2014, so he excluded the public from the courtroom on day 5. That should not have happened.

In the end, is a small formal trial error really the reason why Smith is able to return to a life of freedom?

CHAPTER 6:

Sudden infant death

The inscription on the richly-decorated tombstone of a child's resting place moves the passing visitors: "Darling, we miss you." Nothing is worse than losing your own child. When you can't see your little one grow up, with all the ups and downs that life brings with it like first love, graduation, and marriage. While some may ponder these thoughts, other mourners notice something else - the sun-drenched cemetery of Bovina, Texas has five such gravestones on its barren green areas and everyone has the same inscription: "Darling, we miss you".

Diana Lumbrera was born in 1958 in Friona, Texas, the first child of 25-year-old Antonio and 19-year-old Juanita Lumbrera. They are Latinos who have always been suspiciously-eyed by the "whites" in the

United States. Life is not easy for the Lumbrera family as the mouths of seven children need to be fed. Perhaps Diana is particularly in need of love, and desperately requires more attention from her parents, but as eldest she quickly grows up and takes responsibility for the younger ones, despite feeling uncomfortable in this role.

Diana enjoys it to the fullest when she is sick, because she receives the full care and attention so vital to her and for which she yearns so much. Perhaps this is the reason that the girl's burgeoning hypochondria is encouraged? At the age of 13, Diana is already perfectly capable of pretending to be ill and getting everyone to feel sorry for her. But a desire for independence and freedom, a strong need to get one's own way and satisfy one's own needs eventually leads to Diana being thrown out of school.

Antonio and Juanita, dreaming of social advancement like everyone else in the U.S., are appalled and blame their teenager. The adolescent girl has had enough of it and quickly decides to leave home. Without further ado, she marries Rodolfo Carrillo. She is only 14 years old and Rodolfo is only 18, but her parents give their consent because they are simply happy to get rid of the girl who, in their opinion, is completely off-track. But just one year later, Rudolfo throws in the towel and leaves Diana. However, this is the moment when her fate makes a decisive turn. In 1974, she meets Lionel Garza, the man who will be the father of her first children and whom she later marries.

The first to be born is Melissa, the daughter in whom Diana may recognize herself. She loves the girl very much and doesn't want to be separated from her at all. Everyone around her is touched and impressed by how a girl who used to be so wild could become such a wonderful, caring mother. Although Diana is only 16 when she gives birth, she slips seamlessly into the role of the loving, tender mother, who picks every wish from her offspring's eyes and adores the little girl.

No one is surprised that Lionel and Diana quickly conceive their next child and a year later, Joanna is born. A beautiful girl with whom the proud parents attract many glances. Diana does everything she can to live up to her dual responsibility. And although caring for an infant and a toddler learning to walk is a real challenge, no one hears a single nasty word from her. The young woman is completely absorbed in the joy of motherhood.

On November 30, 1977, a heavy blow shakes the small, homely, family world of Diana and Lionel. Both live happily together, although at that time a marriage without a marriage certificate is still offensive in conservative Texas.

The emergency room doctors and nurses interrupt their work for a moment as the heavy front door pops open and a completely disbanded, loudly sobbing petite woman runs in. In her arms, she holds a small bundle – an infant, apparently, which she presses close to herself. She screams, cries and begs for help. Joanna, her beloved Joanna, has stopped breathing! Screaming that she had cramps before and that they have to help her, the hospital staff reacts seamlessly and with lightning speed. Indeed, the 3-month-old infant is lifeless and no longer breathing. Immediately, everything is arranged for a resuscitation. All pray that it is not too late! Again and again they start with the resuscitation attempts, while in the background the desperate young mother cries and sobs. But despite the doctors and nurses' best attempts, they finally realize that they can't do anything for the little girl anymore. Slowly, their grey, exhausted faces turn to the mother and the leading doctor shakes his head. It's too late.

Transitionless, Diana begins to scream again - this time in pain and anger. She accumulates accusation after accusation against the helpers, accusing them of simply not having tried intensely and long enough. They just let her baby die! Although some nurses take the woman, who is beside herself, aside and explain to her that *Sudden Child Death* unfortunately happens from time to time, Diana Lumbrera struggles to calm down. Her obvious, deep suffering affects everyone. A pathologist subsequently confirms that the death was a suffocation resulting from previous convulsions. With that statement, he closes the file and an autopsy is not carried out.

That same year, Lionel Garza and Diana Lumbrera

commit themselves to marriage. He too suffered greatly from the suffocation of his little daughter. Maybe the marriage is his desperate attempt to make up for something, to end the constant quarrels with Diana and hold the rest of his small family together. Gradually, Diana begins feeling better and slowly begins to participate in life again - at least until February 10, 1978.

That day, the young woman appears again in the hospital, this time in Bovina, and carries her son, Jose, just two months old in her arms. He had severe cramps, then his breathing stopped she tells the doctors and begs them to save her Jose. She cannot bear another loss of a beloved child! This time the little child still shows weak signs of life and in fact in this case, the resuscitation of the infant succeeds, everyone can barely believe their luck. To rule out complications and find the cause of the cramps, little Jose is transferred to the pediatric intensive care unit in Lubbock, but no one can find anything unusual. All the data suggests Jose is in good health.

Then on February 13th, an alarm signal sounds for the first time from his little bed. The children's nurse immediately runs to Jose, only to see Diana withdraw from his crib. According to the clinic staff, he was doing well in the afternoon, at least until Diana calls her husband and tells him that his son is dying. Shortly after 6:30pm, the infant actually dies and immediately afterwards his mother runs out of the room in tears. Still, no one suspects anything. Rather, everyone feels terrible for the poor suffering woman who has to endure so much.

Then, just 8 months later, similar scenes play out at the municipal hospital of Bovina. On this day, Mrs. Lumbrera arrives at the emergency room with her firstborn, Melissa, now three years old, and calls for help. This time, the child in her arms is already dead and the resuscitation doesn't change that. Again, Diana describes mysterious seizures as the cause of suffocation. According to pathologists, the child has suffocated from swallowed vomit.

Diana divorces Lionel in 1979. For some, it looks as if the young woman finally wanted to end her misfortune. Later, it is said that she was very superstitious and believed in curses and evil spirits. A friend even reports that her mother-in-law cursed poor Diana, causing her so much misfortune.

Over the next 7 years, Diana will have 3 more children and will lose them all. None will grow old enough to see the inside of a kindergarten classroom. Again and again she talks about mysterious cramps that are said to have caused the death by suffocation. And again, everyone feels sorry for the poor mother.

Finally, not even the children of her relatives are safe anymore. Is the mother-in-law's curse possibly spreading and circling? On 8 October 1980, the 6-week-old daughter of a cousin dies - again as a result of cramps, and still nobody is suspicious.

A total of 7 children die and the oldest is just four years old. This child, of all the children, results in the end of this terrible series of deaths. This time the police were called into the hospital. When they finally start an investigation, the shocking truth comes to light - a truth many of Diana's relatives and acquaintances still today don't want to believe.

Jose Antonio was born in 1986. He alone manages to survive. At 4 years and 3 months, he gets the usual cramps and is taken dead, by his mother to a hospital, allegedly so that he can be resuscitated there. But this time, someone gets suspicious. Why? The day before, Diana took Jose Antonio to the pediatrician where she told the doctor her usual story. He wrote a prescription for an antibiotic which, as the investigation reveals, was never filled. This visit, and numerous other pediatrician appointments, are later seen as a clear indication that Diana had planned her actions thoroughly and for a long time to counter potential suspicions.

But when Jose Antonio dies, a wary hospital employee finally draws the right conclusions and alerts the police. The responsible detective starts with an interrogation of Diana and begins to collect and list the events of the past years. Seeing his notes in black and white in front of him, the man becomes rigid with horror. Could it be? Is this woman, who earns her living as a meat packer, really more of a monster than a mother?

Now, the districts of Palmer, Lubbock and Castro are

also beginning to investigate. It turns out that for each of the deceased children, a life insurance policy had been taken out in the amount of between $3,000 to $5,000. For Melissa, the policy amount was even increased shortly before her death. That was a lot of money for a Latina at the time. Diana was not inactive financially, as the prosecution soon finds out that she invented Jose's alleged leukemia and his father's death to get an $850 loan through her employer and a credit union official. Were all these murders just for money?

More evidence against Diana is that no one but her has ever seen her children's alleged convulsions.

In Garden City, Palmer County, Lubbock County and Castro County, Lumbrera is finally charged with the murders of her own children and her cousin's daughter. The first verdict is passed after less than an hour of jury deliberation. She is sentenced to life. The Texas Rangers continue to fly the murderous mother to her next trial and back again. In the end, Diana Lumbrera, who probably suffered from a particularly serious variant of the so-called Münchhausen syndrome, receives a total of three life sentences. Her aunt Elodie nevertheless asserts, "She was a loving mother and she took care of these children".

CHAPTER 7:

The holiday replacement

D ixon, Illinois, is about 150 kilometers from Chicago. It is proud to be the birthplace of U.S. President Ronald Reagan and tractor manufacturer, John Deere. It is poetically referred to as the "Petunia Capital of Illinois". It is also a typical American small town. Here, the clocks tick differently. With just 16,000 inhabitants, virtually everyone knows everyone, from school or work, which is why one's own gut feeling is the decisive criterion for judging people when dealing with one another. This also applies to Rita Crundwell, who everyone saw as a pleasant, modest and reliable woman.

A similarly-friendly simplicity existed in Dixon with regard to the administration. Instead of having a city council system with control mechanisms and a division of tasks, the honesty of the citizens who stood for election was always the main focus. For a long time, the city government consisted of a part-time mayor and four city councilors responsible for the various departments. In most cases, less value is placed on technical knowledge than on the fact that the person is "a nice guy". So retired teachers, sports coaches, real estate agents and other honorable citizens got their chance. Most had rather little idea about administration or bookkeeping. In fact, for a long time Dixon had something quite naïve about it. The attitude prevailed that everyone is good and wants only the good for each other, at least until the day when a huge coincidence revealed that $53.7 million was missing in the city's treasury.

Rita Crundwell, née Humphrey, was born in 1953, one of six children in a busy working-class family. However, Ray and Caroline Humphrey are distinguished by one thing - their love for horses. More precisely, quarter horses, a typical Western horse breed which develops an immense speed on a quarter mile. The Humphreys even managed to win a few prizes for their self-bred horses at regional shows.
This special love for the quarter horses is what will drive Rita Crundwell throughout her life. Her dream will be to turn the modest breeding on the family farm into something of special significance.
When the teenager is 17 and performing an internship at Dixon City Hall, Rita realizes that she also enjoys this work. After high school, instead of studying, she starts a full-time job in the city. The

young woman is clever, capable and committed. She quickly familiarizes herself with the subject and gradually develops into the heart of the financial administration. Everyone is full of praise for Rita, who masters the subject perfectly in a very short time. She is always friendly, courteous and willing to help in any situation. In 2011, a former member of the city council will even say, "She is an enrichment for the city. She cares about the city budget as if it is her own".

In her free time, Rita continues to breed horses intensively. When she is in her twenties, she already achieves her first successes at breeding shows. Later the woman from Dixon will even be called the "Queen of Horses".

But first, she makes her professional career progress. At 33, she becomes Dixon's controller and financial administrator. She has an excellent reputation and appears to be perfect for the vacant position. In her private life, she is also doing very well. Two years later, she wins the Quarter Horses Championship in Indiana and shortly afterwards, in Texas. But this is only the beginning of her meteoric rise in the horse breeding scene!

In the following years, Rita increases her horse breeding from one or two dozen horses to several hundred. She buys large estates and carries out extensive reconstructions. She then buys another farm in Wisconsin, led by her partner. Beyond that, she rebuilds the inherited, detached house into a 325-

square meter luxury dwelling with swimming pool, buys extravagant clothes and jewelry as well as a luxury mobile home with marble worktops, tiled floors and, believe it or not, five televisions. The "Queen of Horses" drives to breeding shows with her numerous assistants in a fleet of same-colored vehicles, where she performs, and everyone knows and adores her. Rita Crundwell wins a total of 52 World Championships with her horses. Nothing happens in the quarter horse's business without Crundwell.

Nobody in Dixon is aware of any of this. Now and then a little note about Crundwell's successes is published in the regional newspapers. She still works her modest job in the financial administration for a salary of just $80,000 a year. In Dixon, it is believed that Rita earned a great inheritance long ago and thus, that's how she initially financed her lifestyle. Later, the citizens just assume that horse breeding is very profitable because at some point, Rita Crundwell's breeding success becomes well-known.

As she spends more and more time at shows, she is often given time off from her work. She even offers to forgo her salary for a time, something that is noticed benevolently. Furthermore, Rita is always available when on tour by e-mail or telephone if questions arise in the administration. Everything looks as if she is the kind of employee anyone would wish for.

But she also has to make unpleasant decisions. In 2008 when the global financial crisis kicks in, Dixon is hit hard. When the city purse is almost empty and payments from tax revenues by the State of Illinois are delayed, Crundwell's analysis makes it clear that drastic cuts are the only way Dixon can survive. Many employee benefits are cut and one third of the road maintenance department is laid off. Other employees receive no pay rise for at least 3 years. And yes, it will even be necessary for the citizens to make a donation to continue. Surprisingly, Rita's personal lifestyle is not affected at all, but yet her façade doesn't crumble. No one has any idea that Rita is the reason why the city and its inhabitants are in such a bad state.

In 2011, as the financial crisis subsides, Crundwell is once again on the road when her temporary replacement accidentally stumbles across a strange detail. Kathe S. is a city clerk and one of just three administrative officials. She wants to prepare the monthly cash report and finds that there are no statements yet from the Fifth Third National Bank for a special account. When Kathe S. receives no feedback on her written request, the city clerk calls the bank, slightly annoyed, and demands that she be sent a statement for every account the city has in the bank. When she finally receives and thoroughly-reviews the documents, the administrative officer becomes suspicious. She has never heard of an account called "investment reserves sewerage system". Maybe that's why she takes a closer look and is surprised to find that this account always receives astonishingly high amounts, sometimes in the six-figure range! Then Kathe S. discovers something else, which is even more strange. Someone allows the expenses from his personal credit card to be debited from this municipal account. She finds debits from petrol stations, department stores and much more. When Kathe S. reads the cardholder's name, she can't believe her eyes - Rita Crundwell.

Totally shocked, the city clerk keeps the matter to herself at first. She doesn't know what to do. After all, the two sit close together at work. She shudders at the thought of what Crundwell has done and suspects that she is using the secret account for her horse breeding. A few days later, Kathe S. speaks confidentially with the mayor, James B., in his office, who is also completely aghast. Both decide in their helplessness to call in the FBI.

Both are asked not to let anything of their suspicions get out to the public while the investigation is in progress. This lasts for six months, but when the facts are finally on the table and the full extent of Rita Crundwell's embezzlement becomes clear, the FBI decides it is time to act.

On Tuesday, April 17, 2012, the officials enter Dixon City Hall inconspicuously and go directly to the mayor's office. The mayor calls Rita Crundwell into his office and leaves her alone with the FBI agents. The intensive interrogation lasts two hours, after which, the "Queen of Horses" leaves the town hall in handcuffs, never to re-enter again.

Perhaps it was because Dixon's citizens were stunned and appalled that something like this was apparently possible in their city, but the trial proceeded incredibly quickly. By 14 November 2012, Crundwell had pled guilty to transfer fraud, probably to prevent worse, and was sentenced to 19 years and 7 months in prison.

During the course of the trial, the full extent of her fraudulent activities is revealed to be the largest case of embezzled community funds to date. On average, Rita Crundwell embezzled about $2.5 million a year for more than two decades in a city that only generated $8-9 million a year.

For a total of 22 years, between 1990 and 2012, Crundwell enriched herself at the expense of the state by transferring a total of $53.7 million from city accounts to the secret sewerage account she set up for this purpose. Initially only small sums were transferred, but in the end the sums became higher and higher. Her method was actually quite simple. Crundwell booked tax revenues due to the city of Dixon on a real public investment fund. She then drew up invoices for a fictitious investment project and paid the amount by cheque into her secret account. Rita Crundwell invoiced non-existent projects and then paid the invoices to herself. As financial administrator, she is entitled to sign all payment orders herself and at the same time, release them for payment. Nobody controls her.

The 177 invoices were miserable forgeries with typos, missing contact details and the obligatory coat of arms of the State of Illinois. If someone had taken a serious look at it, it would have caught their eye immediately. But that never happened, neither by Clifton Gunderson's auditors commissioned by the city, nor by the small accounting firm that later took over the audits. However, it turned out that Rita Crundwell had a very good personal relationship with Clifton Gunderson. She even played on the company's softball team. Her personal accountant, who prepared her tax returns and administered the income generated by horse breeding, was again on Clifton Gunderson's payroll. And for the accountants' slovenliness, they even billed the city of Dixon one million dollars.

In October 2012, a lawsuit was filed against Clifton Gundersen, the small accounting firm and the bank. The court granted Dixon a total of $40 million in compensation. The auction of Crundwell's horses and the sale of her real estate and valuables raised another $12 million, which the city also received.

In response to this incredible economic fraud, the citizens of Dixon decided at a 2016 city meeting to set up a transparent administrative system with functioning supervisory bodies. The overthrown "Queen of Horses' began to remain silent after the trial.

CHAPTER 8:

The Preacher

When the operator at the emergency call centre answers the incoming call at 0:43 am, he only listens with half an ear. He is tired, as the night shift is always long and exhausting. But there's something in the voice of the telephone line that makes him sit up and take notice. The voice sounds well-modulated, full and strong but with an undertone that resonates latent panic. He politely introduces himself as Walter Railey. When the operator asks him what's going on, his answer is, "Oh, I just got home and my wife's in the garage. Somebody did something to her."

The operator freezes at this sentence. He has worked there long enough to suspect that something terrible must have happened. He confirms by asking, "Was she beaten up or what happened? His fingers are already twitching towards the emergency but-

ton, and it's the right idea because the caller's answer brings terrible certainty, "I don't know. She' s foaming out of her mouth or so ...".
The emergency call operator reacts immediately because someone is fighting for her life with all her last strength!

In 1987, Reverend Walker Railey was already a national figure as the rising star of the Protestant Church in the U.S.A. He preaches on radio, publishes books and is considered a hot candidate for the 1988 bishop election. That would make him the youngest bishop in America. With his stirring sermons, he fills church halls and more and more people discover their faith and join the congregation in downtown Dallas. The medium-size man with the steel-blue eyes, who is already becoming bald, comes from simple circumstances. The son of a tin worker, he grows up under unsightly conditions. His parents are alcoholics and therefore, often neglect their offspring.
Nevertheless, he manages to develop into an admirable preacher through an immense inherent energy and tenacity. To live up to his high expectations, he works on a sermon for up to 35 hours and has a staff of 65 assistants around him. Some colleagues are beginning to fear that Railey considers himself to be the voice of God. Again and again, he is advised to seek psychological help to cope with the increasing stress level.

Presumably the fierce temperament smoldering within him is the inevitable flipside of his energy. The more he gets professionally, the more stress he's under, and the clearer his choleric side becomes. Even the smallest events can cause a violent eruption. A perfect example is if the lighting in the church is not right. But while many choleric people apologize for their outbursts, Walker Railey seems to simply be moving onto his daily routine. Yes, it even seems as if he feels some kind of icy satisfaction afterwards.

His 38-year-old wife, Peggy, is very different. The reserved woman is a musical person. She sings in the church choir and plays the organ with absolute virtuosity. It is here where she blossoms.

The unequal couple have two children together, five-year-old Ryan and two-year-old Megan.

Dallas is known for employing the best paid preachers in the whole nation. The city can proudly boast 1,200 church congregations. Walker Railey earns a respectable $100,000 a year. When Pastor Railey received the first threatening letters in March 1987, everyone initially suspected it was a reaction to his criticism of racism, for he repeatedly denounces social grievances in his speeches. He does not shy away from condemning the death penalty, pleads for gender equality, thematizes an ambivalent view regarding abortion, and even advocates for the rights of homosexuals.

The temporary climax in the matter is set by the

mysterious lines on Easter Sunday in which the preacher's downfall is prophesied. This Easter Sunday is an important day. Among the listeners is not only Peggy Railey, listening to her husband, but Lucy P., a woman with special meaning for the spouses, sitting right next to her. After all, the handsome blonde psychologist and daughter of Railey's great role model, Bishop Bob Goodrich, is his mistress. Some in the congregation suspect a relationship between the two - but what does Peggy know? Is she completely unaware or does she know that she is sitting next to her rival? At this moment, the concern for her husband's and children's father's life takes up too much space to be able to give room to doubts and rumors.

But everything goes well, and things stay calm. Nobody suspects that only two days later, on the night of April 22, 1987, everything will change. Shortly after midnight, more precisely at 0:43am, the police receive the emergency call. A man asks urgently for help because "someone has done something to her". On the line is Reverend Walker Railey who found his wife, Peggy, in the garage unconscious. When they ask what's wrong with her, he explains that she has foam in her mouth. Obviously, the otherwise eloquent preacher is completely overwhelmed by this situation. In front of him on the floor lies his wife, whose body is convulsively twitching due to severe brain damage.

Walker also calls John and Diane Y. They are good

friends of the family and John is an important mentor. Then, Walker looks after his children. He finds them safe and sound in the house. Fortunately, they didn't notice the crime committed against their mother in the garage. Megan lies in front of the TV, while Ryan sleeps soundly.

When they finally arrive, the paramedics are shocked by Peggy's condition. Her face is bluish and swollen and her neck is broken. Obviously, someone strangled her with extreme brutality. But the odd thing is that there are no signs of a fierce fight, as would be expected from an attack by a stranger. Peggy's glasses are still on her nose, her hair is neat and not tousled. Already at this point a terrible first suspicion appears - did she possibly know her attacker?

Before Walker Railey follows the ambulance, which rushes away with sirens and blue lights, he asks John and Diane, the godparents of his children to take care of them.

In the days that follow, the events will be hasty. While Peggy is in the hospital struggling with death in the intensive care unit, she becomes a topic in the church congregations. Everyone rages against the potential author of the threatening letters. As a result, hundreds of visitors come to the Presbyterian Hospital to pay homage to Peggy, almost like a saint. At the same time, her condition is devastating. Because of the choking, her brain got too little oxygen, while at the same time it was "flooded" with glucose. Even if she survives, large parts of her brain are so badly damaged that only a breathing body remains.

The day after his wife is admitted to the hospital, the minister, accompanied by a lawyer friend, goes to the police and tells his version of the evening. However, this will be the last time he talks directly with the police.

According to Railey, he arrived at home on April 21st at about 6:30pm, where he talks to his wife in the garage over a glass of wine.

She's about to grease the garage door because it's so hard to move. A short time later, he drives - in a business suit - to the library because he wants to work on the footnotes of his latest book. At 6:38pm, he calls home and leaves a message on the answering machine. He states the time, although it is generally known that he never wears a watch. At 7:26pm, he calls the babysitter to discuss something for the weekend. Four minutes later, Railey contacts his mistress, Lucy P., and then drives to her, allegedly to get tapes of relaxation exercises, and stays for about 40 minutes. The preacher then returns to the library to devote himself again to his studies.

After 8pm, he approaches an employee in the Bridwell library and wants to know the end of that day's opening hours. At half past eight, he calls Peggy again and shortly after that, he leaves the library again and drives off in his car. Around 8:53pm, he shows up at a gas station in Greenville to refuel and buy a wine cooler.

A jogger next sees a conspicuous man in a suit running away from the Raileys' house around 9:30pm. Neighbors also report that between 10:15-10:30pm, they hear strange noises coming from the street behind the house of the reverend and his family.

But what actually happened in the time between shortly after 9pm and 0:43am?

Walker Railey claims that he was thirsty and therefore, had to go to the gas station. Immediately after that, he went to the Southern Methodist University Library to do more research. According to him, a librarian with whom he was still in contact could prove this.

In the course of the following week, however, the policemen begin to doubt Railey's version of the evening, as more and more inconsistencies emerge. His alibi - a visit to the Southern Methodist University Library - stands on clay feet because there is evidence that Railey is not telling the truth about the period between the visit to the gas station and his conversation with a librarian sometime between 11pm and midnight.

Strangely enough, at midnight, he provides his business card to a Nigerian student with a message for the librarian written on the back - along with the time when the note was supposedly written - 10:30pm.

When he leaves the library, he picks up the phone and allows himself to be connected directly to the answering machine, without it first ringing in the house. Strangely enough, he leaves another time - a wrong one. Records from the telephone company show that the call was made three minutes after midnight. The message is that his wife should quietly close the garage door. He parks outside. Oddly, Railey also stresses that he is not wearing a watch. On the one hand, it's well-known that he never wears a watch and on the other, his wife probably knows this fact best.

At 0:29am, another call is placed on the answering machine, again mentioning the time and that Walker Railey is finally coming home. Eleven minutes later, he arrives at his home and finds the garage door half-open. The garage is dark, because strangely enough, the light bulbs above the automatic door opener have been removed. The minister enters the garage with his headlights on and discovers his wife on the floor behind her Chrysler.

The policemen quickly get the uncomfortable feeling that someone is trying to create a waterproof alibi to get himself out of the line of fire with the investigation, which makes them all the more suspicious.

On Sunday, after the terrible attack on Peggy which has put her into a coma, a service is held for the first time again in the Raileys' church. The preacher allows a message to be read from him, stating "I do not know why senseless violence continues to penetrate society, nor do I understand why the events of the past week took place".

Nine days later, the police visit Walker Railey in the hospital, because the evidence becomes more and more overwhelming. They want to ask him important questions. However, the police officers are standing in front of a locked door. Since he doesn't react to the knocking, they gain access to the preacher's hospital suite by other means – and just in time! With difficulty, the unconscious man can still be saved. It appears he tried to commit suicide, as the long note next to his bed explains. He took three bottles of sedatives and antidepressants. As a reason, he writes in his farewell letter that for years there has been "a demon" in him who has always been there. "People have seen me as good. The truth is just the opposite. I am the baddest of the bad."

A few days later, the preacher wakes up from his coma. In contrast to Peggy, who will never wake up again. Even though his lines may seem like an indirect confession to many, the Dallas police still don't have enough evidence to prosecute Walker Railey. Instead, the prosecutor urges him to "move his life". He actually returns his license to preach, leaves his children to their godparents and moves to California in 1987 where his lover, Lucy P., had already moved before him. The two now live together.

Peggy's parents have not stopped trying to hold Railey accountable and even filed a civil suit. The verdict was pronounced in absentia because Railey does not appear. He is ordered to pay $18 million in compensation. Later, the punishment is converted into lifelong monthly financial support for Peggy.

Finally, in 1992, investigators were able to prove that Railey wrote the threatening letters himself. In addition, the files regarding the attempted murder are finally closed. The trial in San Antonio fails because of rivalries between the two assistants to the Attorney General. In the end, Walker Railey is acquitted.

Four years later, he separates from his mistress and meets a widow, Donna B. He succeeds in obtaining a divorce from Peggy and marries the widow in 1998. Railey does not invite his children, his mother or his brother to this wedding. He will remain silent about the incidents for the following years. As time goes by, the gifted rhetorician opens his mouth again from the pulpit. He continues to fascinate his audience with his sermons to this day.

The children, Ryan and Megan, now live in Houston and have had their surnames changed. They have broken off contact with their father. Peggy dies in December 2011 without speaking a word in 25 years, leaving many questions unanswered.

What actually happened on 21 April 1987 and who is Walker Railey really? An innocent man, wrongly suspected or has he actually taken his own children's mother? A voice from the afterlife calls for justice, but no one is willing to answer.

CHAPTER 9:

Blackout

The factory worker with the brown hair and blue eyes has little time. His well-deserved coffee break is scarce. Hastily, he sips the hot coffee to dispel the tiredness. He is tall at 1.98 meters. He surpasses everyone in the diner. A man sits next to him, watching him stealthily while pushing chewing tobacco from one cheek to the other. Obviously, he wants to get rid of the tobacco. When the worker is finished, the friendly stranger asks him for the paper cup, which he hands. The tall man then leaves the diner. He no longer sees that the paper cup carefully disappears into a plastic bag for evidence, which his neighbor carefully closes with a beaming smile.

Faryion Edward Wardrip was born on June 3, 1959 in Salem, Indiana as the fourth child of nine. His parents are ordinary people. His father, George, is a factory worker, and his mother, Diana, earns some money as a cleaner. She is the organizer in the family who sets the tone when needed. They are simple people who love their children and support them to the best of their ability. Although there may be disagreements at times, Faryion has a close relationship with his parents and they will always be his safe haven to return to.

However, teenage years are a difficult time for everyone, and the young man is constantly arguing with his father. He is also experimenting with marijuana for the first time. Over the next few years, drugs will play a decisive role in his life. This starts in high school, causing Faryion to need to leave school before he can graduate. As a result, he joined the National Guard in 1979 at the age of 19, and was accepted. Everyone hopes that the strong military structure will exert a good influence on him, but he cannot adapt. In the end, Faryion is dishonorably discharged for smoking marijuana and repeatedly staying away from duty without permission.

Did his parents already expect it? For the young man to be standing at their door again and seeking shelter with them? But regardless, they don't turn him away; after all, it's their son. When the family moves from Indiana to Wichita Falls in Texas, Faryion comes with them. Perhaps he's hoping for a new start as well.

And in fact, something will change here in the long run. It's here that he meets the woman who will make a lasting impression on his life, in good times as well as in bad. Faryion Wardrip is 24 years old when he meets 20-year-old Johnna D. Jackson. In March 1983, the two of them get married, hoping for a happy relationship for the rest of their lives. Quickly, two children are born but Faryion's drug problems quickly catch up with the young family. He can hardly get through the day without drugs and alcohol, but this has a strong effect on his behavior. When the young father and husband consumes intoxicants, he becomes extremely aggressive and angry and beyond that, violent and assaulting.

The determined Johnna, however, is not impressed by this. She continues to put her husband under increasing pressure. She demands that he finally find a permanent job to get the family through as the revolving door of jobs must stop! So far, Johnna's parents have repeatedly needed to support her financially. Apparently, Faryion Wardrip is actually intimidated by her, because he takes a janitor's job at the Bethania Hospital in Wichita Falls. He is quickly promoted to hospital porter. Nevertheless, the fierce quarrels between him and his wife do not stop, often ending with countless accusations and insults.

Later, Faryion Wardrip will confess to how incredibly stressful his relationship with his wife felt to him. Yes, it was even traumatic. In 1984, he continues to become completely entangled in his drug excesses, which make his life an ongoing nightmare.

Perhaps it was this fatal combination that eventually demanded a kind of discharge, like a pressure cooker that ends up exploding in a garish fireball.

On the evening of December 20, 1984, Faryion Wardrip once again had a fierce quarrel with Johnna. Enraged, he left the house and walked around to clear his head. That same evening, 20-year-old Terry Lee Simms leaves the hospital at around 11pm. She is petite at 1.60 meters and holds a part-time position as a technical assistant, as well as being a student at the nearby Midwestern State University. That evening, after a shift at the hospital, she and her colleague and learning partner, Leza B., drive to acquaintances in the late evening to exchange Christmas presents. Afterwards, both want to study together in Leza's apartment, but she gets a call from the hospital around half past nine asking her to step in. She gives Terry her apartment key and drops her off at her place.

Leza returns at 7:30am. She rings the bell and knocks, but Terry doesn't open. Is she just sleeping too deeply? Leza gets the key from her landlord, but freezes like ice as she steps into her living room. A hopeless chaos reigns! The young woman calls her landlord for help before she looks further around - perhaps she is afraid of what she will discover in her apartment once she continues looking around. Then, a shock hits them both as they enter the bathroom - in the middle of a huge pool of blood lies Terry's exposed corpse, raped and brutally stabbed!

Her petite hands are tied with a power cord at her back. She had to endure all of this while being completely defenseless.

More murders of young, petite women continue to shake Wichita Falls and the region.

On 19 January 1985, Toni Jean Gibbs, who was also employed as a nurse at the hospital, disappeared. Her abandoned car was discovered two days later, but it was not until February 15th, one day before her 24th birthday, that construction workers found her body in a field one mile south of the city limits. Again, the body is found naked, as Toni Gibbs was also raped and stabbed. There are eight puncture marks, making it seem as if the perpetrator acted out of rage. But the worst thing is that nearby they find an old, scrapped school bus in which Toni's clothes are found. Traces prove that she survived the attack before crawling out into the field to die.

A 24-year-old man, Danny Loughlin, is falsely-accused of the murder. He does not pass the lie detector test, but on the basis of a negative DNA comparison, he is acquitted.

Four days after finding Toni's body, Faryion Wardrip quits his job at the hospital. He moves to Fort Worth, two hours away by car, where he wants to find a new job.

25-year-old Debra Sue Tayler also lives there. Her husband sees her alive for the last time in the early morning hours of March 24, 1985. He leaves a nightclub before her because he is tired and wants to go home to bed. When Debra doesn't come home, he is worried and reports her missing to the police.

On March 29th, she reappears under terrible circumstances. Two construction workers find her body on a construction site. She was strangled. First, the husband is targeted by the investigators, after their relatives draw attention to him. He passes three lie detector tests without a problem, but the prosecutors are still convinced of his guilt. Only years later, will this change.

Faryion Wardrip returns to Wichita Falls in the hope of finding a job in his hometown, as his new job in Fort Worth fell through.

On September 20, 1985, student Ellen Blau disappears in Wichita Falls on her way to her car after her shift as a waitress. Again, the car containing Ellen's wallet is discovered abandoned elsewhere in the city. Her corpse was found by street workers on October 10, 1985, in a field in Wichita County. Tragically, the body is already so badly decomposed that Ellen can only be identified by dental records. The perpetrator's DNA can no longer be found either. Therefore, the cause of death cannot presently be determined. Much later, it will be determined that she was strangled and possibly also raped.

Faryion Wardrip now works in a nightclub and his marriage is definitely over. In December 1985, Johnna files for divorce and a year of separation begins. Whether or not Faryion is relieved about that, he makes no attempt to save the marriage.

He is still heavily-addicted to drugs and alcohol when he befriends a waitress, Tina Elizabeth Kimbrew, in the spring of 1986. At only 21, she was killed by Faryion Wardrip on May 6, 1986. In his drug-fueled madness, he suddenly sees her as his hated wife, Johnna, and completely freaks out. He suffocates the young woman with a pillow. However, Wardrip is observed by neighbours as he leaves the complex. Does he know that or is it a feeling of guilt that determines his next steps?

Wardrip panics and flees to Galveston, Texas. On May 9th, he calls the police in Wichita Falls and threatens to commit suicide. The local police then visit him and Wardrip readily confesses to the murder of Tina Kimbrew.

In October 1986, while Wardrip is in prison, Johnna's divorce finally becomes legal and to his relief, this chapter of his life is closed. In court he pleads guilty and gets 35 years for the murder.

But the time in prison brings a personal change for the man: Not only does he finally manage to leave alcohol and drugs behind and get clean, he also discovers faith. In the end, he is a deeply religious person who is released early on parole on 11 December 1997 on the condition that he must wear an electronic anklet. Wardrip moves in again with his parents in Wichita Falls and turns his life around. Not only does he find a new job, he also becomes actively involved in the local church community, singing in the choir and teaching Sunday school. He also meets the new love of his life, Glinda. On October 15, 1998 the two get married and move into an apartment in the same complex as his parents.

Still the local police are under serious pressure in their search for the murderers of Terri Simms, Toni Gibbs, Debra Taylor and Ellen Blau.

In this case, the importance of good communication and intensive networking of services across city and regional borders becomes apparent. It is highly-probable that the murder cases could have been solved much more quickly with a better exchange of information between departments; however, takes until 1999 before there are any useful findings.

In 1999, detective John L., reopened the investigation and initiated a wide-ranging analysis of the DNA material and sampling of other potentially-suspicious individuals. However, the results still do not provide a hot trace. Only when Wardrip's name suddenly appears during the investigation does the case start to move. However, there are no DNA samples from him. Detective John L. does everything in his power to obtain them. He follows Wardrip for days - in vain. On the 6th day, he finally gets lucky! In the diner, he manages to get the suspect's cardboard cup as a spittoon for his chewing tobacco. Immediately, the detective races into the office and hands over the sample to the laboratory.

Shortly afterwards, Wardrip is called to the police

station, where the man is confronted with the murders of Terri Simms, Toni Gibbs and Ellen Blau. At first, he refuses to cooperate, bur further tests then confirm the result. Finally, he confesses. When he is asked about a motive, it becomes apparent how easily drugs can turn a person into a monster, especially when the victim is incapable of adequately defending himself against a person perceived as overpowering. Faryion Wardrip reports that he was always in a drug frenzy when he killed and that just before the deed, Johnna's face would suddenly appear before his eyes, insulting and humiliating him. He would then black out completely. He could never remember how he killed or whether he raped the woman. According to his account, this was the case every single time. During this conversation he also confesses to the murder of Debra Taylor, which had not yet been connected to him.

On 9 November 1999, Wardrip is sentenced for the four murders. He receives three life sentences. He is sentenced to death by lethal injection in the Terri Sims case. In 2010, the verdict is revised on the grounds that Wardrip's defense was not sufficiently effective. Ultimately, the death sentence is commuted to life imprisonment with no prospect of early release and probation. The earliest he can submit a petition for clemency is after a period of 60 years.

CHAPTER 10:

The house

Some houses seem to attract misfortune. There are bad accidents, separations, tears, deaths or even murders. While one door further down, the world is fine. Are they really always pure coincidences or is there a hidden negative energy that attracts evil like a black hole devours planets? People who believe in the supernatural call such buildings haunted houses, while others see them as an excellent opportunity for a lucrative real estate business.

In the southern United States, in the State of Mississippi, there is such a negative house. More precisely, it's located in the Yazoo district, in the small town of Vaughan. It's here where the Hargon family plays an important role. A one-story brick house originally accommodated a shop belonging to the Hargon clan. Haywood Hargon owned Fowler Road Grocery until a fateful Friday in 1994. Suddenly, a man with a gun stood in front of him at the grocery store and demanded his weekly income. A total of $114 was the reason Haywood Hargon died. The thief fled when another customer happened to enter the store.

After Haywood's tragic death, his son, Michael, inherited the brick building on Fowler Road in Vaughan and converted it into a residential building. It included a small nest for his family - his wife Rebecca, two years older, and his young son, James Patrick. Maybe he kept the house out of respect for his father's memory or to prevent it from falling into the wrong hands. His uncle, Charles Hargon, was worried that his adopted son, Ernest Lee Hargon, might get his hands on it. In fact, Charles was downright afraid of what would happen to the house if Ernest owned it because, as one relative pointed out, no Hargon blood flowed through Ernest Lee's veins.

The adoption happened because Charles Hargon married Ernest's mother and raised him as his own child, but the relationship between the two was marked by highs and lows, mostly by lows. Maybe Ernest Lee was not good enough for him, because he "only" worked as a truck driver for a livestock transport. It was a power-sapping job with long working hours. For this reason, Ernest Lee starts taking methamphetamine at the age of 40 to avoid falling asleep while driving. The quarrels between father and adopted son escalate so much that in 2001, Ernest Lee cuts off all contact with his stepfather for the next three years and he doesn't call him back when Charles asks for it in early 2004.

Maybe Ernest Lee was also deeply struck by the fact that Charles got closer and closer to cousin Michael during this three-year break. Their relationship is so close, in fact, that in the end he even replaces Ernest Lee as his son. The two "real" Hargons are so close at the end, that the adopted son is finally disinherited. Now, after Charles' death, Michael is supposed to get the 20-hectare cattle farm in Madison County, a painful development for Ernest Lee.

One thinks of the usual quarrels in a small town, family dynasty, but what follows will shake Vaughan to the core more than anything before.

In this small town, everyone knows everyone. That's why on Saturday, February 14, 2004, pedestrians notice something strange at Michael Hargon's home. The door of his house is open and so is the door of his car - but no one can be seen. At some point, someone gets concerned and walks onto the property, shouting loudly for Michael and Rebecca, but it remains quiet. That's when the concerned neighbor finally goes into the house. The sight that appears before him seems ghostly - it's as if someone has simply "beamed" the residents out of the building in the middle of their daily lives. The dishes from dinner are still standing in the sink, things are on the table, magazines are lying around - but there isn't a human being anywhere to be found. Suddenly, however, the visitors find bloodstains and bullet holes in the walls where the cartridges are stuck, and they realize that something terrible must have happened. Something is not right here!

For the next 17 days, local police and members of the Hargon clan intensively search for the small Hargon family. Nowhere is there a trace of the 27-year-old Michael, his 29-year-old wife and their 4-year-old son James Patrick.

The only suspects are members of the street gang who were behind the murder of Haywood Hargon. The perpetrator back then belonged to the group called The Black Gansta Disciples and a few days before the disappearance of the small family, the possibility of an amnesty was once again examined. Michael had emphatically rejected this request, nevertheless there is no indication that it was some kind of revenge by the Street Gang. The investigators were only interested in the gang because two or three people were supposedly seen in front of the brick house on the morning of Valentine's Day arguing with Michael.

Leap day finally brings a turning point in the investigation. On February 29, 2004, the Smith County police unexpectedly arrest a man. It is Ernest Lee Hargon who is imprisoned for possession of weapons and violations of the Narcotics Act. But on the following day, there is sudden movement in the case of the disappearance of the Hargon family as Ernest Lee is targeted by the prosecution and charged with murder.

Indeed, the day after the indictment, police in Smith County, some 100 km away from Vaughan, make a horrific discovery. As the rain streams, they feverishly search for something with spotlights on the property of Ernest Lee's neighbor. They finally find what they are looking for - the bodies of Michael, Rebecca and their little son lying in a flat, hastily-excavated grave over which sheet metal was laid. All were horribly battered, including the toddler!

What nobody in Vaughan suspects at the time was that Ernest Lee Hargon confessed immediately after his arrest that he shot his cousin and killed his family as well, providing the investigators with the information as to where to find the bodies.

The local and now trans-regional media are furious. Everyone wants to know what new developments took place and what exactly happened, but the police are still holding back in their communication. They want to wait for the autopsies before announcing anything more precise. Rightly so, because the details in this case are difficult to bear, even for the hard-boiled investigators. The jury of nine women and three men, who hear the whole truth about the disappearance of the little Hargon family during the court hearings, is certainly in a similar position.

Before sunrise on Valentine's Day 2004, Ernest Lee drives his 1974 Corvette to the house on Fowler Street. He is very upset and disappointed and full of blind hatred. There is no other way to explain what follows. He walks onto the property and enters the house. A fierce fight breaks out between Michael and Ernest., The prosecutor's assistant testifies to the jury that "Michael suffered injuries all over his body, from his head to his toes". The 27-year-old man is able to flee outside to his truck, as his knocked-out teeth next to the open car door prove. Maybe he was hoping to get the gun out of his car. But before that, he is killed with a shot to the head. But Ernest Lee's revenge doesn't end here, as he can't give up until the last member of this family is out of the way. Initially, he shoots Michael's wife in the arm, hits her on the head and strangles her to unconsciousness. The four-year-old James Patrick is also strangled until he faints. Whether the two have already suffered a broken skull at this time or later is unclear. Next, the man begins to remove any trace of them. First, he hoists Michael's body into his car, then he lays the unconscious wife and the child on top. He drives with them to his residence 100 km away to make them finally disappear. Mother and child are still alive when they arrive at their destination in Smith County - but not for very long. While Ernest strangles Rebecca, she holds her child in her arms. Immediately afterwards, Ernest strangles little James Patrick with a leather sling - but the child doesn't even scream, as Ernest Lee notes in his confession, almost surprised. During the prosecutor's report about the child's death, Ernest Lee Hargon begins to cry.

After killing all members of the hated family, he put their bodies back into his car and drove to the place he later tells the police about. There he buries the bodies and returns home.

He has arranged to meet his wife, veterinarian Lisa A., for a Valentine's dinner at a Mexican restaurant. At first, Hargon acts as if nothing has happened, but eventually can't help but confess to the murders.

Throughout the entire trial he doesn't make any statements, he simply remains silent. Also, his defense team doesn't call any witnesses - even the usual character witnesses are missing. The evidence shows that the trigger for the terrible act was probably Charles Hargon's change to his will. During the course of the trial, two wills are introduced into evidence - one from 1995 and one from January 2004. In the earlier version, Ernest Lee is still listed as an heir, but in the changed last will, his name has completely disappeared from the document. instead Michael is listed as the sole heir. Charles Hargon died at the age of 78 on January 16, 2004 - a few weeks before the murders. For the investigators one thing was certain, the change of the last will and testament is the reason why three people died.

In December 2005, the jury does not need long to reach a verdict - guilty. This means the death penalty for Ernest Lee Hargon, who appears completely emotionless during sentencing.

While others sometimes wait decades for their execution, the fate of the murderer of the three Hargons finally strikes completely unexpectedly and comes before the death penalty. On August 28,

2007, an imprisoned gang member breaks out of his cell in the high-security wing of the Mississippi State Penitentiary in Parchman. Ernest Lee is on cleaning duty when he is fatally wounded by 30 stabs from a homemade knife at 8:53am. He dies in the prison infirmary.

Michael and Rebecca Hargon's one-story brick house still exists today, but nobody wants to live in it anymore because too many people have died there. A barbed wire fence is supposed to keep intruders away from the quiet building, which looks like a giant tombstone.

CHAPTER 11:

Infanticide

For the detectives in the house, the sight they witnessed will never be forgotten in their whole lives. Even the oldest, most experienced investigators, who have seen many terrible things in their years of service, are unable to withhold the tears. There's blood everywhere! Some have to fight the gag reflex. The brutality of the attack is just shocking - who in the world is capable of such a horrible thing?

Each of the three victims lie unnaturally twisted on the ground, their bodies littered with countless puncture wounds caused by kitchen knives. The attack on the youngest child, little Melissa, was carried out with such force that one of the knives actually broke off in her neck. Her skull was smashed in with a kitchen chair. The mother, Joan Heaton, lies in the hallway and looks as if she has been lacerated.

But that didn't seem to be enough for the perpetrator, who was apparently out of control. Only after he had brutally beaten and strangled her, could he let go of the girls' mother.

As the sight squeezes their throats, investigators wonder who is capable of doing such a thing. Is it even appropriate to call such an unconscionable killer a "human being"?

The city of Warwick in Rhode Island is somewhere you can eat mussels and spend wonderful days on the beach. But by the end of the 80s, the idyllic city will be famous for a human monster.

On the night of 21 September 1987, the 27-year-old Rebecca Spencer will no longer see another sunrise when a burglary takes place at her home.

The crime scene in the Buttonwoods district the following day is a terrible one, as the young woman is covered with bleeding wounds. The medical examiner finds a total of 58 puncture sites, a number that amazes and shatters him at the same time. Like a madman, the burglar stabbed the woman in the living room again and again with a box cutter knife. That knife was only accidentally in the house that day because Rebecca was moving and had to pack boxes.

Although the police vigorously search for the perpetrator, the investigation is unsuccessful. Nobody has seen anything striking and nobody has noticed anything. The file remains open, but it becomes quiet around the case. Eventually, the daily business continues; that is, until all are once again torn in a brutal manner from their deceptive serenity.

It is 4 September 1989, two years after Rebecca's death, when Marie B. decides to look for her daughter, single 39-year-old Joan Heaton. She hasn't heard from her for a few days and is a little worried. Marie is also looking forward to seeing her granddaughters again, 10-year-old Jennifer and 8-year-old Melissa. Together with her other daughter, Marie heads to the Heaton's house.

Arriving at Buttonwoods, they see Joan's car parked in the driveway, so she must be home. The two women ring the bell several times, but nobody opens the door for them. They are irritated. Joan and her girls usually storm to the door immediately, so Marie and Mary Lou decide to enter the house.

As soon as they enter the hallway, they immediately realize that something is wrong! Everywhere they look, from the furniture to the walls, there are blood splashes. A rotten stench overcomes them, like dead animals that have been lying around for a few days. Their fear is increasing. What happened here? As they move on, the women make a discovery that could not be more horrible! First, they find Joan. Her body lies in the hallway, covered with blood-stained sheets. Jennifer lies nearby, also brutally murdered. The youngest, Melissa, they find in the kitchen.

As soon as they are able to think clearly enough, they call 911. A few moments later, the investigators arrive. The Heaton house, once filled with laughter, has turned into a crime scene and everyone agrees that this was the playground of a human monster.

During the course of the following investigations, one thing quickly becomes clear – Warwick has a real serial killer. The resemblance between the 1987 case and the murder of the Heaton women immediately stands out to the detective; nevertheless, the police can't make sense of it and are at a loss. In which direction should they investigate? To not waste valuable time and out of concern for the citizens of Warwick, the police request the help of the FBI. They send one of their best profilers, Gregg M., and he immediately goes to work summarizing the available evidence and quickly deduces that both crimes were committed by the same perpetrator. In both the Heaton and Spencer cases, the murderer used a weapon that was present in the house. This fact suggests that he must have invaded for some other reason - perhaps a theft? Was he surprised and then grabbed the first available weapon? That's the profiler's guess. Also, the "overkill" in both cases - about 60 stab wounds on the bodies of the mothers and 30 on the children - indicates that that it was the same person that committed both crimes.

On this basis, the profiler is also certain that the burglar must come from the neighbourhood of the victims. Burglars tend to break into houses where they know they can get something valuable. And as a rule, neighbours know each other and their living conditions best. In this respect, it is very likely that the perpetrator also comes from the district of Buttonwoods.

But it is the FBI specialist's last assumption that will eventually lead the detectives on the trail of the merciless killer. Gregg M. assumes that the perpetrator has most likely injured himself in his completely uncontrolled attacks.

The policemen take a deep breath. Thanks to these clues, the field of investigation is clearly narrowed. Now all they need is a little luck.

On September 5, fate provides a helping hand to the Warwick police. Just one day after the discovery of the Heaton bodies, two patrol officers, Ray P. and Mark B., drive through a park near Buttonwoods and pass a teenager already known to them for some break-ins, 15-year-old Craig Chandler Price. They stop the car to talk to him.

Craig was born 11 October 1973 and is a tall, lively teenager with a winning smile. Ray P. knows him privately because he coached him in a basketball course. That's why he knows that the colorful boy lives in a small ranch house in Buttonwoods. When the policeman approaches him about the murders, it turns out that Craig Price lives only a few houses away from the Heatons. Ray P. and his colleague also hold their breath as they see that the young colored man has a bandaged hand! Only with great difficulty do the men manage not to reveal their suspicions directly. Can it really be him? Price claims that he was injured when he smashed the window of a car last night. He nobly leaves out how he apparently wanted to steal the car.

In the following days, the policemen review Craig's story and discover interesting things. For example, nobody reported a broken car window and there are no glass shards to be seen at the place mentioned. Nevertheless, many in the department believe the two are just wasting their time; after all, Price is just a teenager. However, he is a teenager with a criminal record and a penchant for violence, which is why he becomes a potential suspect for the two detectives.

When he is summoned to the police department, he is first interrogated intensively, especially about the injury to his hand. Since Craig insists on his version, he is subjected to a lie detector test which confirms that he is lying. However, nothing can yet be proven. The investigation becomes more serious when they discover that Craig usually hangs out with a gang of teenage burglars where he boasted of a very special act - the murder of Rebecca Spencer.

In the early morning hours of September 17th, the Price family's house is searched by the police with a court order. John Price, Craig's father, is completely shocked when he sees the policemen on his doorstep. The same is true of Craig's mother and brother, who are required to stay in the living room during the search. Only Craig is surprisingly and completely relaxed, even falling into a deep sleep on the sofa. However, it doesn't take the policemen long to discover something important. In a garbage bag they find six bloody kitchen knives, like those in the Heatons' house. Furthermore, there are bloody clothes and gloves, among other things.

Craig and his parents are immediately taken to the police station to question him again about the murders. What happens next shocks everyone deeply. The teenager suddenly willingly admits to having murdered the Heatons. Completely calm and relaxed, he describes in detail exactly what happened during the night. Has lying and denying become too tedious for him? In a nonchalant way, the 15-year-old high school student reports on the evening. Intoxicated to the brim with marijuana and LSD, he entered the house to steal something he could sell for money. As he tried to crawl in through the open kitchen window, he fell onto a table in the kitchen. The deafening noise startled the Heatons. He reports how he violently hit the mother as he stabbed her. And finally, as a macabre punch line, he imitates the last sounds of the dying girls.

Craig's father, John, gets sick when he hears his son's story. He finally has to run to the men's room and vomit, unable to return. His mother, standing next to her son the whole time, suddenly sobs painfully from deep within her chest. What has become of her little boy? What went wrong in childhood that made a teenager so cold-blooded and capable of such heinous deeds?

When Craig Price is asked about Rebecca Spencer, he also admits to this murder without hesitation.

At that time, he was just 13 years old and still a child himself. The teenager obviously still remembers every single detail of the crime. He doesn't seem to experience repentance or anything like it.

In the end, silence fills the police station. What words would be appropriate in view of these deeds? Detective Tim C., who conducted the interrogation, goes home that night to cry. He was the first to arrive on the scene of the crime. Assisting Detective Kevin C., he feels nothing but cold anger because he already senses what will follow and he would be right. Over the next few years, he does everything in his power to change the law, but for now he has no choice but to accept it. Craig Price may already know that the law of Rhode Island is on his side. Maybe that's one of the reasons for his relaxed, outspoken confession. He is arrested one month before his 16th birthday - and is therefore considered a minor. His "timely" confession means that, despite the extremely brutal murders, he does not have to answer to a court or serve a prison sentence. After just five years in an educational institution, he will be free again and his criminal record will be deleted. At 21 years-of-age, he will be a free man with a clean record.

It looks like a dreadful prophecy and warning as Craig Price triumphantly proclaims at the end of his hearing that, "He'll write history when he's 21 and free again!" And almost sounding amused, he muses that he will smoke a "bomb" (i.e. a strong hallucinogen like LSD or mescaline) when he comes out after five years. The tale of Craig Price proves that one is capable of doing bestial things under the influence of drugs!

It is decided at the hearing that Price will remain in custody at the Rhode Island Training School's Youth Correctional Center (YCC) until his 21st birthday. It is here that he graduates from high school and starts attending college courses. Craig Price is aiming for academic honors, but repeatedly comes into conflict with the law - he obstructs the ordered psychological analysis and therapy, repeatedly lies to the psychiatrist, and threatens an officer of the educational institution by blackmailing him. Craig Price himself torpedoes his chances of quickly living in freedom again. A court finally decides to imprison him for 15 years because of the incidents. That means that the "Warwick Slasher" will remain in custody even after his 21st birthday. During the trial, the young man has a tantrum and rages, claiming that everyone is lying to cause him problems. The judges are only the heads of a conspiracy directed against him!

And even this punishment is no warning to him. Several times he is involved in prison fights and attacks on the guards. Last but not least, in 2009 Craig Price receives another 25 years in prison for almost fatally injuring a fellow inmate with a homemade knife. Everyone breathes a sigh of relief as this postpones his release until 2020.

Detective Chris P.'s efforts, meanwhile, have led to

changes in Rhode Island's law. Never again will it be so easy for young people to evade their responsibility for serious crimes. Craig's sentence will finally be served in December 2020, when the formerly youngest serial killer in the United States will be released again at the age of 46 years.

Psychologists are confident that he can't be rehabilitated. The FBI and Warwick police believe it's only a matter of time before the Warwick Slasher starts killing again.

Price sees himself as a victim of continued racism. This racism and his enormous frustration about it were the reason for the "overkill". He never gets tired of stressing that he has already been punished enough.

CHAPTER 12:

The Party

Tyler Hadley from Port St. Lucie is initially a very nice, uncomplicated and even shy, child. He is born as the second child of Blake and Mary-Jo Hadley, six years after his big brother. He is very close to his parents, and laughs and jokes with them often. At the age of 10, he quarrels with his mother. Tyler is so angry at his parents that he tells a neighbour, Mark A., that he is going to kill them, but the neighbor doesn't think he's serious. There is another boy, Mike M., who will stand by Tyler as his faithful friend for the next several years. The two share an unbreakable friendship.

Life in the small town of Port St. Lucie is not spectacular, especially for teenagers preferring to leave all boundaries and conventions behind. The narrowness of such a city can be depressing. Blake and Mary-Jo, two particularly pleasant, friendly people, like living in their beautiful house, which Blake finances through his work at the local power plant. They strive to be good, caring parents who pave the way for their children and accompany and support them to the best of their ability.

At the age of 15, Tyler's nature suddenly changes, and everyone blames it on puberty, which is in full swing. The teenager doesn't want to go to school anymore, hangs out with the wrong people, and starts drinking and taking drugs. Above all, Tyler likes smoking marijuana, which is not hidden from his parents who are convinced that this is just a phase that will pass. Nevertheless, Blake and Mary-Jo try everything in their power to accompany Tyler through this "crisis". They want to help him. This includes visits to a psychiatrist, who prescribes anti-depressants to the teenager. He also participates in an outpatient program for mental health and drug abuse.

How must this all feel for Tyler Hadley? Does he get the impression that he's under someone else's control? Does he feel forced to do something he doesn't want to do? Does he think that he is being portrayed as sick and crazy, even though he only wants to live a life he thinks is good? Maybe he really felt that way, but maybe not. The only known fact is that none of these efforts are successful. Tyler Hadley becomes more and more rebellious and only isolates himself further from his parents. It's more important to him to be seen as the cool teenager who is the center of attention and he would do almost anything for it.

At 17, the boy is arrested for serious assault and burglary. When Blake and Mary-Jo Hadley hear about this, they are shocked. Obviously, none of their previous relief efforts have helped. In their desperation, they consider out loud whether it wouldn't make more sense to have Tyler committed to a psychiatric ward. They can't see any other way of saving their beloved son, but he's no longer on board with their attempts to help him, especially with his hatred for his parents growing almost daily in him. In the Spring 2011, he says things on several occasions like: "I hate my parents," or "I hate my mother and would love to kill her". At a family reunion in mid-July of the same year, however, he seems completely normal to everyone present.

A new low is reached when Tyler comes home drunk in his car two weeks before the party that will make its mark in history. To protect the 17-year-old from himself and to punish him, his parents take his car and smartphone away from him. He is placed on house arrest. Incredibly angry, he writes to a friend that he would like to kill his mother.

On the morning of 16 July 2011, the day of the fateful party, Tyler writes Matthew, another student at Port St. Lucie high school, at 9:40am. He is still flirting with the idea of a mega party that will be remembered throughout Port St. Lucie forever. In the chat, it reads as if the party was meant as a kind of reward - a bonus for the death of his parents, who only annoy him. Matthew even jokes about it and goads his friend, about murdering his parents. Tyler has been expressing these thoughts for quite some time now, so his friend probably thinks that his classmate is all talk and not serious. Matthew most likely isn't aware of how determined his friend can actually be - with fatal consequences, and his parents are completely unaware of his dreadful desire.

The thought of doing something awful to his parents gets more intense every day for Tyler Hadley. On Friday, he shocks Mike M. with the statement that he allegedly stood at his parents' bed the night before and considered killing them. And on Thursday, he told his friend, Markey P., who is playing PlayStation, that he wants to murder his parents and then celebrate with a mega party. Markey thinks it's a bad joke, because Tyler says that nobody has ever done anything like this before. He wants to have a party while the bodies are still in the house.

At noon on July 16th, the Facebook post appears inviting everyone to a party at Tyler's parents' home. He reaps confused reactions and asserts that nobody has to worry about his parents. They would not come home, as they are allegedly in Orlando, Florida. These statements somehow irritate Mike M., especially after Tyler's strange sentences from last night.

At 8:15pm, the confirmation is sent, the party is definitely taking place, and everyone is invited. What happened next is difficult to determine. Probably shortly before 5pm, Tyler steals his parents' cell phones to avoid them making an emergency call. It seems like a bit of irony and a reaction to his phone being taken away from him as punishment a few weeks prior. Whether he swallows the 3 ecstasy tablets because he lacks the "courage" for the upcoming crime is unclear, but he waits until the drugs take effect and then gets himself in the mood with the song "Feel Lucky" by rapper Lil Boosie.

Finally, the desired kick hits and Tyler gets up, goes into the garage and gets a claw hammer that hangs by the tools. With the cool grip of the heavy hammer in his hand, the teenager walks into the living room of his parents' house where his mother is sitting at the computer. He stands there for 5 long minutes, waiting and staring at the neck of the woman who gave birth to him, and then he strikes. He hits his mother with the full force of the hammer on the back of her head. As he smashes his mother's skull, she screams, "Why?

His father hears his wife's screams and comes running from the master bedroom. It's as if he is walking against an invisible wall when he sees Mary-Jo lying on the floor with her head smashed to pieces. His son, with a hammer in his hand to which blood, hair and shreds of skin still stick, stares into his father's eyes until he can only get out, "Why?" "Why the fuck not?" Tyler then hits his father on the head with the hammer until he is dead as well.

Immediately afterwards, the teenager begins to

clean up. He wraps the shattered heads of the corpses in towels and drags them to the master bedroom, where he throws them onto the bed. Then he piles pictures and various other objects on his murdered parents. Downstairs, he removes the blood. It takes 3 hours to get the house ready for the party.

Then the guests start to arrive. About 60 people show up, most of whom Tyler doesn't even know. They party, play beer pong, smoke cigarettes and drink. The party is a real success, but Tyler seems tense and stays in the background. Around 7:30pm, Mike M. finally arrives. After some time, Tyler asks his friend to come outside because he has to discuss something with him.

Outside the door, Tyler confesses, "I murdered my parents." Mike first thinks his buddy is kidding and doesn't believe it. He points to all the obvious evidence. His mother's car is still outside the door, his father's is in the garage. There are traces of blood, for example, on the computer keyboard. Some guests have already noticed both. Nevertheless, Mike still doesn't believe his friend. It's only when Tyler presents him with the bodies in the master bedroom that he becomes convinced.

What follows now seems incredible. Mike doesn't go directly to the police, but instead shoots a selfie with his friend and continues celebrating. At the party, the story that Tyler killed his parents gets around because he alludes to it again and again, but everyone seems to think it's a joke or doesn't care.

Mike leaves the party early in the morning and finally reacts. He alerts the organization, Crime Stoppers, which immediately informs the police. At 4:40am, just as Tyler posts about another party at his house that evening, the police arrive at his front door.

In 2014, the verdict is pronounced, and Tyler is given a life sentence without the possibility of probation for first-degree murder. The crime was planned and deliberate. The judge even describes the 17-year-old as "dangerously anti-social". During the trial, the defense attorney points out that the boy was suicidal and drugged. An expert adds that young people up to the age of 25 cannot yet fully assess their behavior or its consequences. But Tyler himself confesses that he's guilty, emphasizing only that he can't explain it to himself. Since then, the rest of the small Hadley family has been split, with his own brother pleading for Tyler to receive the maximum sentence.

In 2015, one appeal was successful due to an insufficient discussion of an alternative to life imprisonment. In 2016, the decision is taken to withdraw the verdict from the first trial and start a new trial. Two years later, Tyler Hadley apologizes for the murder of his parents for the first time . He is repeatedly found guilty and sentenced to life imprisonment, but this time, he is given the opportunity for probation.

CHAPTER 13

The Intruder

(by Alexander Apeitos)

It is shortly after midnight on the evening of 5 June 2002, when the unimaginable happens - 14-year-old Elizabeth Smart is kidnapped from her bedroom. For months, the girl seems to have disappeared from the face of the earth. Then, on 12 March 2003, after nine months, Elisabeth suddenly reappears.

Elizabeth Ann Smart was born on 3 November 1987 in Salt Lake City, Utah. The second of six children of an architect and a housewife. Her parents make every effort to support the child, who has a special artistic talent. Elizabeth discovered her passion for playing the harp at the age of 5 and has been practicing every day for several hours ever since. She is a friendly and smart, but shy child.

She gives concerts at secondary schools and is booked as the harpist for weddings and annual autumn concerts. In addition to her love of music, she is also an enthusiastic horse rider and participates in various tournaments. Elizabeth attends Bryant Intermediate High School, where she receives an award on 4 June 2002 for her special athletic fitness and outstanding academic performance. She is a really uncomplicated child. That same evening, Elizabeth's whole family is present to celebrate her school success. After dinner, as she prepares to go to bed, no one suspects how terribly the peaceful life of this model family will suddenly change.

Elizabeth shares a bedroom with her younger sister, Mary Katherine. On that evening, the two girls talk until they fall into a deep sleep. By midnight, the house has become completely quiet. Everything is dark and all family members are asleep. Nobody notices when a darkly-dressed man carefully approaches the house. There is an open window, so it is easy for him to enter the house noiselessly. He heads straight for Elizabeth and Mary Katherine's bedroom. The intruder is armed, holding a knife firmly in his hand. He places the ice-cold, matt-glittering blade on the neck of sleeping Elizabeth. With his other hand, he closes the girl's mouth.

"I have a knife. Don't make any noise now," he hisses threateningly at Elizabeth. The girl needs a moment to slowly wake up and realize that the man is not part of a bad nightmare. She feels the cold metal on her carotid artery in a beating manner. "Get out of bed and come with me or I will kill you and your whole family," the man commands.

Elizabeth obeys - out of fear for her life and out of fear for the life of her beloved family. She moves as slowly and as quietly as she can. She carefully gets out of bed and follows the stranger out of the house and into the garden, dressed only in her pajamas.

The dark burglar leads Elizabeth behind the building and walks toward a nearby hill. She walks along without resistance, is rigid with fear and can't get a sound out. The teenager doesn't even dare to look around because the whole time she feels the cold steel of the knife in her back. Elizabeth doesn't know how long they walk. Time stretches in these moments of extreme tension, and minutes become hours. After the girl and the kidnapper have crossed the hill, he leads her into a small forest, where he abruptly stops, as they have arrived.

A tent can be seen in the middle of the small forest, with plastic tarpaulins spread out on the floor. Behind the tent, a large hole yawns in the forest floor, which is mostly covered with tree trunks and dirt.

Where am I? Why am I here? What does this man want from me? Will I ever see home again? Such questions are racing through Elisabeth's head incessantly in the moment. She is just trying to put her thoughts in order when a woman steps out of the tent.

She comes straight at Elizabeth, grabs her trembling

hand and pulls the girl behind her into the tent. There, she forces her to sit on an inverted bucket. In the dirt, spiders and mice can be seen.

The woman suddenly begins to pull on Elizabeth's pajamas, but Elizabeth resists and refuses to be undressed. Again and again she asks the woman, through her tears, what they want from her and begs to be let go. The woman is silent, relentless and does not abandon Elizabeth. Finally, Elizabeth explains that she just wants to undress herself. She also makes it clear that she bathed before going to bed and doesn't need to be washed again.

Without saying a word, the woman hands the girl a robe and lets go of Elizabeth. Then she picks up the pajamas from the floor and leaves the tent. Elizabeth cries. She is so full of fear that she almost vomits.

How is my family? Did the man kill them? What will he do to me? These thoughts are circling incessantly around the head of the kidnapped girl.

Then the tent door opens, and the unknown man comes in. He has also changed his clothes and is now wearing a white robe. He approaches Elizabeth, kneels in front of her and tells her that she will now become his wife and must fulfil her marital duties.

Her kidnappers are the 49-year-old Brian Mitchell, a self-proclaimed prophet self-named Immanuel, and his wife and student, the 56-year-old Wanda Barzee. That Elizabeth has met her kidnapper before, she will notice later.

<u>The kidnappers</u>
Brian David Mitchell was born on 8 October 1953 in Salt Lake City as the third of six children. His parents, Irene and Shirl Mitchell, are Mormons and educate their children according to the strict rules of this religious community. At the same time, the father confronts the children with pornographic photographs at a very early age in order to teach them how to have sex.

Generally, his educational methods seem rather strange. To teach Brian an important life lesson, Shirl abandons the 12-year-old boy in a completely unknown neighborhood and instructs him to find his way home alone. The older Brian gets, the more he isolates himself from his environment. His relationship with his parents is extremely poor and at the age of 16 he is sent to juvenile detention because he got naked in front of a child.

After his release, Brian is sent to live with his grandmother. Here, he comes into contact with drugs and alcohol, which he begins to consume. Finally, the young man quits school. At 19, he leaves the state of Utah and marries Karen M a 16-year-old girl. During their two-year relationship, two children are born. Custody is granted to Brian after their separation because Karen is heavily-addicted to drugs.

In 1980, Brian's life takes another radical turn after a spiritual conversation with his brother. As a result, Brian joins the Church of Jesus Christ of Latter-day Saints. This community is considered a splinter group of the Mormons and is the third largest religious community in the U.S.A. after Judaism. The following year, he marries his second wife, Debbie. She brings three children into the marriage and together they have two more. After only a few months, they are taken into a foster family. Brian files for divorce in 1984, claiming Debbie is violent towards him and the children. Debbie, on the other hand, says that Brian has changed from a gentle man into an insulting, aggressive, controlling husband. According to her, he tells her what to wear and what to eat, and his enormous interest in Satan is frightening.

After the divorce, Debbie reports to the Youth Welfare Office that Brian raped her 3-year-old son, however, this abuse cannot be proven.

In the same year, Debbie's daughter reports something similar. She claims to have been raped by Brian for several years. Also during this time, Debbie reports her ex-husband to the police, but it never comes to a charge. The same day Debbie and Brian divorce, Brian marries 40-year-old Wanda Barzee.

Wanda Barzee is a single mother of six children who has left her ex-husband. Shortly after marrying Brian Mitchell, she moves in with her children. Generally speaking, Brian and Wanda's children get along well at first, but as time goes by, they become more and more uncomfortable around him due to his strange behavior. Brian's view of religion also gets more and more extreme. One night, he wakes up his stepson and tells him that he has just spoken to angels. In 1990, he changes his first name to Immanuel ("God is with us"), leaves his church, and calls himself a prophet of God.

Wanda becomes Brian's disciple and presents herself as the "jewel of God". In the winter of 2001, the couple moves back to Salt Lake City, to the same neighborhood where the Smart family lives.

<u>The first rape</u>

After Brian has finished his wedding ceremony, he coarsely pulls Elizabeth down from the metal bucket she is sitting on and throws her to the floor. He rips off her robe and starts raping the fourteen-year-old teenager. Through her tears, Elizabeth keeps begging him to stop and let her go, but it doesn't help. Rather, it seems as if her despair and begging only stimulate him further.

When Mitchell is finished, he leaves the raped Elizabeth lying huddled on the tent floor. The young girl finally falls asleep, exhausted by the ordeal. When Elisabeth wakes up, Mitchell is already present and kneeling over her. Again he rapes her, then wraps a thick metal cable around her foot and attaches the other end to a nearby tree. Elizabeth is now his prisoner and unable to escape her tormentor. Whenever he desires it, she is forced to give herself to him - often several times a day. When she dares not do what he asks, she is beaten violently and sometimes even tortured. Elizabeth is forced to drink alcohol

and take drugs to become more compliant. Sometimes, she receives nothing to eat or drink for days
in a row. There is also no toilet or shower in her
prison. She spends the first few months in only the
tent, chained up and repeatedly subjected to abuse.
Apart from that, she spends most of her time in the
tent waiting and pondering. Every now and then,
Brian preaches to her for hours about his mission
and his faith. He talks several times about the fact
that he wants to kidnap and marry six more girls
in the name of God. The turning point comes when
completely unexpected. Elisabeth is almost ready
to surrender to her fate, when the self-proclaimed
prophet is sent to prison for a week after shoplifting.
Elizabeth and Wanda Barzee are on their own. Meanwhile, Elizabeth believes that she will die of thirst.
She hasn't had any water to drink for several days.
Then, a heavy downpour comes down by chance and
the two women can alleviate their thirst. This unexpected rain probably saved their lives.

When Brian Mitchell returns to the hideout, he eases
the conditions of Elizabeth's imprisonment a little as he is already very sure of her submissiveness.
As a result, she is even allowed to accompany him
into the city. During these trips, Elizabeth is hidden
under a long robe, her face is covered with a veil
and she is forbidden to talk. When she is approached
one day by a policeman in a library, she unexpectedly has an important chance to be rescued from the
violence of her tormentors, but the girl is so intimi-

dated that in the face of freedom, she doesn't get a word across her lips. Elizabeth silently walks past the policeman and accompanies Mitchell back to the hiding place.

On 12 March 2003, after 9 months in the tent, Brian Mitchell and Wanda Barzee leave their hideout with Elizabeth and return to the city. They feel safe enough to want to find a new place to stay.

Elizabeth is disguised to make her unrecognizable. She wears a gray-haired wig, a long robe, a head-scarf and sunglasses. Together, the three offered an extremely strange sight, so all eyes involuntarily turned towards them. As a result, the unbelievable happens! Is it a hint of fate or does heaven personally intervene? A passer-by thinks he recognizes Eliza-beth Smart as the strangely-dressed woman and alerts the police.

A few minutes later, the trio is stopped by the po-lice. It takes several minutes until Elizabeth finally summons up all her courage and is able to answer the question about her name. Although Mitchell is still trying hard to get rid of the policemen, the cop urges the disguised woman to answer. And finally, her lips form the redeeming sentence, "I am Eliza-beth Smart!"

Her tormentors, Brian Mitchell and Wanda Barzee, are arrested on the spot; however, it will take 7 long years until they are finally sentenced in court. After the arrest of Mitchell and Barzee, various ju-dicial and extrajudicial hearings, hospital stays and psychiatric examinations of the couple follow. Experts consider both perpetrators to be incapable of guilt. Brian Mitchell refuses to make any statements about the kidnapping of Elizabeth Smart. Again and again he begins to sing hymns in the courtroom, causing the hearing to be postponed.

After Wanda Barzee was ordered to take medication, she is finally brought to trial in 2009. She pleads guilty to the accused acts and is sentenced to 15 years imprisonment. On the other hand, Brian Mitchell, sticks to his tactic of not being able to stand trial. Elizabeth Smart, however, does not give up. She convinces the court that he is faking his mental illness. After all, Mitchell will be on trial again in 2010. On December 11th, the verdict is successful. The jury sentences Brian Mitchell to life imprisonment 7 years after the crime.

Today, Elizabeth Smart is a young woman with a mission. Shortly after returning to her parents' home, she returned to school, graduated and studied music at Brigham Young University. She also committed herself to helping victims who have experienced similar crimes, and is involved in writing the U.S. Department of Justice's Handbook of Assistance for Abduction Victims.

Elizabeth Smart is now a prominent figure in U.S. media, encouraging other victims and helping them get back to a normal life. In interviews, she talks about her experiences in a vivid and detailed way and addresses the question of whether there were any opportunities for her to escape her kidnappers. These possibilities actually existed. The most important reference to Elizabeth's kidnapper came a few weeks after her abduction, from a family member.

Her sister, Mary Katherine, was awake in bed the night of the kidnapping. She was frozen in fear, unable to move, but she will never forget the silhouette of the kidnapper. And one day, she actually knows who it reminds her of - a craftsman who occasionally worked in the house of the Smart family. His name was Immanuel.

But nobody could have guessed at the time that Immanuel was actually the kidnapper of her sister, Elizabeth. Another time, Elizabeth heard her uncle calling for her near her hideout. Often there were helicopters circling around the camp.

But there was always this terrible fear inside of her. The fear of Brian Mitchell hurting her or her family if she dared to get herself noticed. "I decided then that I would live on, no matter what."

Elizabeth is now married and the mother of a daughter. In October 2013, Elizabeth Smart released her extensive memoirs entitled, "My Story". The book describes the kidnapping and founding of the Elizabeth Smart Foundation. It impressively attempts to increase general awareness of kidnapping.

CHAPTER 14

The Gift

Help me! Please help me! The dying woman struggles desperately for breath. She fights against the pain caused by progressive organ failure. Her hospital room in the intensive care unit is dark, and there are life-supporting machines and monitors flickering all around her bed. One shows the weakening and irregular heart rashes, accompanied by the typical sound signal, hurting and booming in the ears. It's an echo that mercilessly indicates how the life runs out of Nancy Dillard's body. At the same time, her husband, Richard Lyon, sits tirelessly at the side of his suffering wife's bed and gives her comfort. When he briefly steps out of the hospital room to regain his strength, Nancy's family doctor, Dr. Ali B., looks for his patient. Has she already slid over into delirium? Does she even know that I am not Richard? the doctor wonders helplessly. Then, the mother of two small children rears her last bit of strength to once more plead, "Please, I do not want to die!"

Nancy Cooke Dillard is born on 6 August 1953 in New York, U.S.A.. The Dillard family belongs to the so-called high society, because "Big Daddy", as Nancy's father, William Dillard, is affectionately referred, is financially independent, and has the best relationships and influential friends in the right places. He has made a fortune through profitable real estate deals. Together with her two brothers, the intelligent and extroverted Nancy grows up in the manner of a typical upper-class family.

Richard Allen Abood Lyon, born 22 April 1957, has a completely different family background. He comes from a family of lower middle class believers. His father is an insurance agent, and his mother works as an assistant teacher. Richard is a pleasant, uncomplicated child who never gets out of line. He is very good at school and also very skilled with his hands. His parents are extremely proud when their son is finally accepted to Harvard Elite University in 1979, where he enrolls for a course in landscape architecture.

One of his fellow students is the slender Nancy with her radiant charisma. It must have been confusing for him that she, of all people, became interested in the young man from a humble background. Instinctively, he thinks he knows that even if Nancy loves him unconditionally, her parents will surely see him for all eternity as only an upstart, a man who has virtually "slept his way" into their line. But the cheerful, unconcerned Nancy manages to dispel Richard's doubts. From now on, the two are inseparable. They work hard and are committed to their projects, leaving them to go to bed exhausted. No matter what they do, Nancy is always the one who has the active part, who thinks through and plans the projects. The more reserved Richard puts his energy into the concrete implementation. At some point, they start writing each other's elaborations. So that no one notices anything, they practice as long as it takes for their handwritings to almost resemble each other. Another special feature is the door sign of their shared student apartment - only the name "Dillard" appears here. Only Nancy answers the phone, because Big Daddy and the other Dillards should not know for a long time that the unequal couple is together.

In 1982, they finally get married and relocate to Dallas, Texas. There, Big Daddy organized a job for Nancy working for a former business partner, Trammell Crow. Richard also finds a job. They rent a two-party house with a large veranda and a garden in the back. At first, it's a rather dilapidated place to stay, but Nancy and Richard gradually conjure up a beautiful, homely place with a thriving garden full of life. A paradise for their two daughters, Anna and Allison, who are finally born. To Richard, they are his everything. He loves the girls from the bottom of his heart. He spends as much time as possible with them, playing and building stables for their rabbits.

The two-party house also houses the journalist, Gayle G., whose little son Shawn often spends time with the Lyons. The relationship between the two families, who live so closely together, is friendly - but very loose. Despite the confinement, everyone tries to preserve their own privacy. Nevertheless, it's obvious to Gayle that something is changing in the relationship between Nancy and Richard. Maybe it's because Nancy is moving up into higher and higher positions and eventually becomes a partner at her workplace, while Richard's career is stagnating. She tells others that her husband is having some kind of midlife crisis. Maybe it's because of the sexual therapy Nancy went into in 1989 because she's no longer interested in an intimate relationship. It turns out that during her childhood, from 1961 to 1967, there was an encounter with one of her brothers that exceeded the extent of normal doctoral games. It was something that the Dillard family swept under the carpet, but still, after the therapy, sex was no longer an issue for Nancy and Richard. In any case, the relationship between the two cools noticeably. Maybe that's the reason why Richard has an affair Tami Ayn G., a young determined woman who works for the same company. He spends more and more time with Tami, only coming home to see his two little girls and to fight the fire ants that have settled in the garden. Because they are so stubborn, they even use arsenic. Nancy is disappointed and angry. She loses her radiant smile and reproaches Richard severely, especially when he empties the joint account to buy his lover a $4,900 ring. Could it be that during their discussions, her parents had always warned her about Richard? Neighbor Gayle is a welcome conversation partner for Nancy during this time. When Richard is away again for days, Gayle witnesses Nancy – who's at first angry, but then becomes increasingly depressed. Sometimes, Gayle even provides Nancy with food and occasionally takes care of the girls.

At some point, Nancy makes up her mind that she finally wants the divorce from Richard. She gets things straight and removes him from her $500,000 life insurance policy - without informing him. Her new determination brings a change, because a short time later he comes back to her. He promises that he will end his relationship with his mistress and not see her again. The life of the Dillard Lyon family seems to be back on track. The garden behind the house blossoms again under Richard's hands, the children laugh, and Nancy seems to be recovering.

At this time, Richard is wooing his wife again and takes care of her as before. He takes her to the cinema and gets her food and drink. She doesn't like the drink he gets her, but he can't help it. Apparently, the machine was contaminated because a strange powder floats on top.

Nancy occasionally feels very sick, so Richard gets and gives her vitamin pills. Everyone hopes that her inexplicable health problems will soon be forgotten. One morning, when a gift basket with a bottle of white wine in it is placed on the veranda in front of the Lyons' doorstep, everyone is happy about the nice, unexpected present - even if the noble donor does not reveal himself. The cork is slightly damaged, but nothing else is noticeable. Several days later, Nancy opens the bottle to drink a glass of wine. Suddenly, on the same day, she feels so miserable that Richard takes her to the hospital. He asks his neighbour to look after the children, and gently assists his wife down the stairs. The doctors at the hospital can't find a cause for Nancy's disastrous condition. Tests are made feverishly to find out why she is getting worse and worse. All the time, the Dillard and the Lyon families are worried about Nancy from different rooms in the hospital. The Dillards and Big Daddy still don't seem to consider Richard's family to be on par with them. Richard watches his wife's bed almost all the time, leaving it only briefly when her family doctor, Dr. Ali B., goes to see her. The husband appears collected, is even seen joking with the doctors. At some point, however, Nancy falls into a coma. While the argument is still raging over whether it is okay for Richard to give the order to switch off the life-supporting machines, Nancy dies. She fights for her life for seven hours, which comes to an abrupt end on 14 January 1991 at the age of 37.

Nancy's death is a severe blow to her children and the Dillard family, especially since their son,

Thomas, died of a brain tumor in 1986. They do everything they can to obtain an autopsy. The result is shocking - arsenic is found in Nancy's liver, kidneys and hair in such a large amount that one thing is immediately clear - she was poisoned! An analysis of the hair shows that there have been several poison attacks on Nancy.

The information is a terrible blow to everyone, and Richard is stunned. But what he does not find out is what Dr. Ali B. reports to the police investigators. When he was in Nancy's hospital room, she briefly took off her respiratory mask and told him about the wine with the defective cork. The Dillards, on the other hand, learn from Nancy's divorce lawyer that she expressed a frightening suspicion in a conversation with her. She believed that she was being poisoned by her husband for some time. As a result, the investigators ask everyone not to mention anything for a while, because the following investigations would take some time.

This succeeds, even if it is a great challenge. Just a few days after Nancy's death, Richard's mistress appears in the two-family house and stays overnight for a while. Six months later, on 2 December 1991, the prosecution finally brings charges against Richard Lyon as the alleged perpetrator. There are numerous indications that speak clearly against him. Not only the statements of his own wife, but also that the dubious vitamin pills taken by Nancy were found by the Dillards to contain poison barium carbonate. Finally, arsenic was found in the garden shed. The fact that he may not have been informed that his wife removed him from her $500,000 life insurance policy also speaks against him. The evidence is growing more serious against the husband, but then the hour of defense follows. They have handwritten letters and diary entries introduced into evidence, all in Nancy's handwriting, as a defense expert confirms.

Among them are some letters that address the alleged abuse by the brother. This also makes him a possible perpetrator. In addition, a partner of Trammell Crow, suspected of embezzlement, is targeted. Was he trying to prevent Nancy from testifying against him? Even Nancy herself is considered a suspect by the defense attorney. Couldn't it have been suicide? After all, she suffered from depression! This is evidenced by invoices for arsenic(III) oxide and barium carbonate, which, according to Nancy's signature, she bought herself. And finally, the fire ants are brought up because these should be fought with the poisonous chemicals.

After these remarks, it actually seems as if Richard Lyon has a chance to leave the court as an acquitted man. The members of the jury are in doubt until the moment another expert is called in - a graphologist and retired FBI official. His statement brings a decisive change. He can prove, with a comparison of writing samples, that the alleged letters and diary entries of Nancy were probably falsified by Richard.

The same goes for the invoices, which the owner of Chemical Engineering Co. clearly identifies as bad forgeries. And even the mistress, Tami Ayn G., contributes her part. She reports that Richard lied to her about the reason for his wife's hospital stay. According to his statement, she allegedly had a blood disease.

The trial ends on 19 January 1992. Jury deliberations do not take long, and the jury pronounces its verdict after only a few hours. In their eyes, Richard Lyon, 34, is guilty of murder by poisoning his wife. He is sentenced to life imprisonment and must pay a fine of $10,000. His motive is still unclear. Many suspect he killed his wife to finally be free for the new woman at his side, without having to sacrifice the comforts of an upper class life. The life insurance policy could also have played a role - if he didn't know that he was no longer the beneficiary, or was he afraid of losing his two girls to the Dillard family in the event of a divorce - with no chance of ever seeing them again?

But what if the latent incestuous relationship with her brother had played a more important role? If the allegedly criminal business partner wasn't the close friend, as Big Daddy thought? Or had Nancy herself been so hateful and determined so as to take revenge on her adulterous husband by committing a treacherous suicide?

The core question of the case was and still is for some: Which graphologist is right?

In 2006 and 2016, Lyon tried to get a parole, but he was denied in both cases. He still asserts that he did not kill his wife. He has also written to numerous legal aid organizations for support, but they have refused to help him.

Nancy leaves behind two children, Anna and Allison. It is not known who took custody of them when their father was convicted and sent to prison. In the meantime, the two have grown up. How difficult it must be to grow up with the suspicion that their loving, caring father slowly and painfully killed their own mother? Did he actually take the risk that his two darlings would become orphans due to greed, jealousy or revenge?

A cruel death is terrible, but hardly anything is as difficult to endure as the uncertainty itself.

CLOSING REMARKS BY THE AUTHOR

Dear reader,

I hope these short stories moved you as much as they touched me when I wrote them. May we all walk the world with attentive eyes for the needs of others and hopefully, prevent many more tragedies.

At this point, I would like to thank my wife, Selina, and my children, Thalea, Matteo and Liana. Many thanks also to Dr. Stefanie Gräf for the excellent cooperation on questions about the psychological background, and help with research and editing.

May I ask you, dear readers, a favor? I come from the south of Germany where we often say with a wink: "Not complained is praised enough". In fact, I have been buying books for years and rarely have I left a positive review. I found many of the books to be great; *however*, I only provided a review if I didn't like something. This gives the negative comments much stronger weight. As an author, I was able to experience how important ratings are in our digital age and how opinions cannot be more contrary. I have decided to leave a rating for every product I purchase, regardless of whether I liked it or not. If you could do the same and provide me with your review, you would help me a lot.

For independent authors, public opinion is very important. Reviews determine the success or failure of a book. It's the readers who decide whether a book is found and read and whether an author can live his dream or not.

My dream is to research more cases worldwide and publish them as short stories. Which country do you think I should dedicate my next book to? Send me your criticism, ideas, feedback and inspiration at AdrianLangenscheid@mail.de and please leave your review before you go. A short statement is more than enough. Thank you so much for purchasing the book. All the best until next time.

Yours Truly,

Adrian Langenscheid

FOLLOW ME ON:

Instagram:

Facebook: https://www.facebook.com/True-Crime-Deutschland-Adrian-Langenscheid

TRUE CRIME GERMANY
Real Crime Cases from Europe
Adrian Langenscheid

Adrian debuted in June 2019. That same month, the *True Crime* book by the as-yet-unknown writer stormed the German Amazon Charts to the No. 1 position in the category of murder. In fifteen short stories, Adrian details some of the most-spectacular German criminal cases of the last few decades. Let yourself be carried away, inspired and moved to tears by these thirteen cruel, but completely unique, murder cases featuring a spectacular kidnapping and a sensational robbery!

Experience the almost-unimaginable pain of the victims and their families! Feel the screaming injustice when the perpetrator cannot be identified or when he leaves the court as a free man! Have fun with an extraordinary robbery that remains unforgotten still today! Put yourself in the position of those involved and marvel at how reality can eclipse even the most-pronounced imaginations!

WAHRE VERBRECHEN: The Podcast by Alexander Apeitos

In the German-speaking True Crime podcast "Wahre Verbrechen", Alexander Apeitos regales us with true tales from "mysterious" to "unbelievable" - it's everything criminal history has to offer. Each episode is dedicated to fascinating new cases. He takes his audience on a criminal journey through time. Alex is not a journalist, detective or forensic scientist, yet you can feel his passion and interest for real criminal cases. He simply can't stay away from real crimes. A growing number of enthusiastic listeners follow him. If you understand German, it's definitely worth listening to!!